WHY STATES?
THE CHALLENGE OF FEDERALISM

© 2007 by The Heritage Foundation
214 Massachusetts Avenue, NE
Washington, DC 20002-4999
202.546.4400 ● *heritage.org*

Printed in the United States of America

ISBN: 978-0-89195-126-1

WHY STATES?

THE CHALLENGE OF FEDERALISM

EUGENE W. HICKOK

Table of Contents

PREFACE   vii

1. WHY STATES?   1

2. THE DESIGN OF FEDERALISM   5

The Constitutional Convention   7
The Bill of Rights   15
A Fundamental Principle   21

3. FEDERALISM AND THE EARLY REPUBLIC   25

Federalism's First Tests   25
The Growing Party Divide   29
The Marshall Court   32

4. A NATION DIVIDED   39

The Nullification Crisis   41
Slavery and Civil War   47
Do States Have Rights?   50
The New Nationalism   52

5. THE ASSAULT OF LIBERALISM   57

The Birth of the Administrative State   60
The Problem of "Incorporation"   63
New Deal Centralization   65
Great Society Liberalism and Its Critics   69

6. THE CHALLENGE OF FEDERALISM   73

Government By Judiciary   75
The Rights Revolution   78
Self-Government and Civic Virtue   83

SELECTED BIBLIOGRAPHY   93

ABOUT THE AUTHOR   95

Preface

It isn't that anyone is really against federalism; that's not the problem. What is of concern is that so few seem to think it is all that important. Everyone knows from their childhood civics— or at least from the moment they try to get a driver's license—that this is a nation of states. So what? Federalism today has become mostly a truism—widely known and accepted but virtually meaningless. In this case, the old saying rings true: Familiarity breeds contempt.

What's worse is that, to the extent that it is taught and studied in the classroom at all, federalism is usually presented as merely a quirk of early American history, and inevitably it is associated with slavery, states' rights, and myriad petty localisms. In short, federalism has suffered at the hands of scholars as much as from the neglect of popular culture. More to the point, federalism has endured popular contempt largely because of its downgrading— along with constitutionalism generally—by liberal historians and academics.

And yet, upon closer examination, it turns out that this overlooked and misbegotten concept is a crucial component of our system of government. What *The Federalist* calls, along with representation and the separation of powers, an "auxiliary precaution" in the Americans' improved science of politics is part of the very infrastructure that makes our political liberty possible.

The argument is rather straightforward. Despite the clear need for additional political authority in the wake of the failed Articles of Confederation, the Framers nevertheless remained distrustful of government in general and of a centralized national government in particular. So while *national* authority was clearly enhanced by the Constitution, the new federal government was to exercise only *delegated* powers, the remainder being reserved to the states or the people. "The powers delegated by the proposed Constitution to the federal government are few and defined," James Madison wrote in *The Federalist*, No. 45. "Those which are to remain in the State governments are numerous and indefinite."

By dividing authority between two levels of government, federalism recognizes legitimate national power at the same time that it provides an added check on the expansion or centralization of the national government and protects a sphere of state autonomy, local self-government, and, as a result, a vast realm of liberty. As Alexis de Tocqueville famously observed, the result is a great open space for the flourishing of civil society, where character-forming institutions—primarily the family, the school, and the church—are free to form the mores and cultivate the virtues required for self-government.

All that said, federalism has had a bad time of it for the last century or so. Indeed, it has been only more recently that federalism has even seen the possibility of revival—a bit in the early Rehnquist Court, and again during the Reagan presidency. Whether the concept has any meaning in modern nation-state politics beyond such exceptions is yet to be seen. What we do know is that any renewal of federalism necessitates a rethinking of the theory and the early practice of American federalism, along with a serious assessment of what gave rise to its steady decline. Hence this monograph, the purpose of which is to make the case for federalism, explain circumstances of its early history and then the assault made against it by 20th century liberalism, and describe how the modern administrative state, the rights revolution, and judicial supremacy have come to take its place—all to the detriment of self-government and civic virtue.

Making that case, and telling this story, is not only an experienced teacher of American political thought but a long-time participant in state and national political life. For fifteen years, Professor Eugene W. Hickok taught political science at Dickinson College in Carlisle, Pennsylvania, twice being awarded Dickinson's prestigious Ganoe Award for Inspirational Teaching. He also served as director of the college's Clarke Center for the Interdisciplinary Study of Contemporary Issues, and was an adjunct professor at the Dickinson School of Law.

In 1995, Dr. Hickok became Pennsylvania's Secretary of Education, responsible for overseeing the state's education system—kindergarten through college. A powerful advocate for parental choice and accountability in education, Hickok helped implement a sweeping education-reform agenda. In 2001, President Bush chose Hickok to be Under Secretary of Education; he became Deputy Secretary in 2004. He is currently a Bradley Fellow at The Heritage Foundation.

This publication is part of a series of essays and occasional booklets published by The Heritage Foundation, under the auspices of the B. Kenneth Simon Center for American Studies, on the "First Principles" of the American tradition of ordered liberty that we seek to conserve "for ourselves and our posterity," as it says in our Constitution. These publications will cover a range of themes and topics, each aimed at explaining our most primary ideas—which often have been forgotten, or rejected—and considering what those principles should mean for America today.

This series is motivated by a powerful observation: Those that lead our nation today—and those who will lead it tomorrow—must *know* and *understand* our first principles if they mean to vindicate those principles and see to it that they once again guide our country.

At a time of continuing centralization of political authority and regulatory power—not to mention ongoing trends in the nationalization of crime and the assertiveness of the federal judiciary—the idea of federalism is all the more sensible, and increasingly attractive. If anything, our experience of governmentalism in the last century underscores federalism's importance not only for our regime but also as an organizing principle for other nations seeking to establish stable democratic constitutionalism in this new century.

Matthew Spalding
Vice President, American Studies,
and Director, B. Kenneth Simon Center for Principles and Politics
Series Editor

Chapter I

Why States?

For many years I conducted a seminar on the Constitution for students completing their studies at the Dickinson School of Law (now a part of Penn State University). Each week we would explore a constitutional principle or theme by reading materials relating to the Constitutional Convention, the writings of the Framers and those authors read by the Framers, and relevant decisions by the U.S. Supreme Court. To start the discussion of federalism, I would distribute a blank map of the United States and tell my students they had ten minutes to identify the fifty states. In all those years, not one student ever succeeded in the assignment. Imagine: Men and women possessing an undergraduate degree and about to possess a law degree yet unable to identify where, say, Missouri is on a map of the United States.

After this exercise, I would ask my students a deceptively simple question: Why states? I would point to that spot on the map where four states touch—the "four corners" of Colorado, Utah, New Mexico, and Arizona—and ask how such seemingly arbitrary borders make sense. The response was always the same. The budding young attorneys would sputter something about history, the division of authority among governments, etc. I would respond by saying I want an argument for the necessity of states, pointing out that an argument for political subdivisions is not an argument for states. My students always had trouble making the case for states. And then we would begin our consideration of the unique American constitutional principle of federalism.

The obvious purpose of my exercise was to drive home the sad fact that few people have any understanding of, or appreciation for, the important role states were to play under the Constitution written in 1787. As we have evolved as a nation and the character and scope of our national government has changed, any popular familiarity with federalism has all but disappeared. As advances in technology have created the means for instantaneous mass communications —we can watch events unfold anywhere, anytime and then must suffer through a seemingly endless succession of talking heads talking about events all the time, anywhere—most Americans know more about what goes on in Washington than what goes on in their state capital (not that they know all that much about what goes on in Washington). In an age in which travel is easy and a time when adults in America relocate an average of seven times, the frame of reference most Americans embrace is defined by what seems to influence their daily lives the most: work, community, national and, increasingly, global events. We reside in states. We are citizens of the United States of America.

The great irony in this, of course, is that the states meant everything in the late 18th century. The men who gathered in Philadelphia to consider changes to the Articles of Confederation, an alliance among the states, came as delegates from their states to act on behalf of their states. The Constitution that emerged from Philadelphia in 1787 was debated in conventions in each state and was subject to ratification by the states. And much of the debate, deliberation, and conversation that took place during that summer in Philadelphia and during each state's ratification convention revolved around trying to understand the relationship that would emerge between the proposed central government and the governments of the several states. What came to be called federalism was at the heart of it all.

And it didn't end there. And it wasn't all talk. The debate about national and state power led, in large part, to the creation of the Bill of Rights. Most of the constitutional controversies during the formative years of the Republic revolved around federalism. Many of the more controversial decisions of the Supreme Court have dealt with federalism. A civil war was fought over the issue. The New Deal was made possible only after the Supreme Court found a way to get around the federalism problems Franklin Roosevelt's proposals presented. And some of today's most contentious issues, such as abortion and gay marriage, are best understood within the context of federalism.

Yet there is perhaps no more misunderstood principle associated with American government and politics than federalism. Generations have lost touch with what federalism is all about. The very term has been maligned and distorted so much that many confuse federalism with the federal government or "Federalists" or "States Rights." Most people equate federalism with intergovernmental relations. But that is too simplistic a formulation. Intergovernmental relations involve the interaction among governments: what goes on between Washington and the states and among the states and their political subdivisions. Federalism is about deciding what *should* go on between Washington and the states; it is about the nature of the relationship between Washington and the states. It is one of the formative issues in the history of this country, its Constitution, and its government.

As a constitutional principle, federalism is important because it speaks not only to the delineation of authority between the national government and the states, but to the overarching concept of limited government and the preservation of individual liberty. Originally, the preponderance of political and governmental responsibility under the Constitution rested with the states. But the Constitution did establish a national government. Tracing the changing nature of constitutional federalism can help us understand how that national government became what it is, and perhaps provide some insight into how we might reclaim those notions of limited government that seem to have faded over time. As a political principle, federalism is critical to the nourishing of citizenship and "civic virtue." Understanding how federalism has evolved over time can help us understand better the nature of our relationship with government in contemporary America, what seems lacking in that relationship, and what to do about it. It can also help us understand the stakes involved in the gradual accumulation of authority by government.

In other words, to understand federalism—as it was and is—is to understand much of the changing character of America—as it was, as it is, and as it might yet be. The purpose of this essay is to set the federalism record straight.

Chapter 2

The Design of Federalism

I n January 2002, President George W. Bush signed into law the No Child Left Behind Act, expanding the role of the federal (national) government in American public education, an area of public policy traditionally reserved to the state and local governments. While there was some talk, primarily at the state level, of invading the prerogatives of the states, few raised that concern as the bill wound its way through Congress. The President, a former governor and self-styled conservative, never spoke about the issue.

In 1986, South Dakota was told it would need to change its laws regulating the consumption of alcohol by residents under the age of 21 or risk losing some or all of the federal highway trust fund money it was due to receive. Up until then, an 18-year-old could purchase a beer in South Dakota, as was the law in many states. Indeed, establishing the policies governing the purchase, possession, and consumption of alcoholic beverages has always been a state function—with the notable exception of Prohibition, and that took an amendment to the Constitution. Suddenly, that was no longer the case. The way Congress chose to exercise its spending powers, attaching strings to the receipt of federal funds, effectively limited the ability of states to regulate in an area which had traditionally been subject to state authority.

In 1973, the Supreme Court of the United States handed down its landmark decision in *Roe v. Wade*. Prior to that, public policy

5

regulating abortions was a matter of state law. Those regulations varied considerably among the states. With this decision, a woman's ability to obtain an abortion became a constitutional right, beyond the reach of state action.

In the early 1940s, Congress sought to regulate how much wheat a farmer could produce, whether or not he was producing it for sale or for home consumption. Relying upon the Commerce Clause of the Constitution—its authority to regulate interstate commerce—Congress enacted policies that touched upon the production of a product, whether or not it was produced for sale (commerce) and whether or not it might be for interstate or intrastate commerce. In 1942, the Supreme Court held that this was an appropriate exercise of Congress's Commerce Clause authority, arguing that even purely private and local activity could be regulated by Washington when that activity might have national consequences. Suddenly, Congress could regulate as commerce activity that clearly was not commercial.

In each of these instances, the nature of the relationship between the national government and the states underwent profound change. In each case, it could be argued, there were important political, governmental, social, and economic issues at stake: issues with national implications that might overshadow individual state interests. And in each case, the authority of the states was diminished—by a President, by the Congress, by the Court. The history of federalism in America is illustrated well by these actions. But that certainly was not what those who wrote the Constitution expected.

It is surely an overstatement to say the Constitution is merely a bundle of compromises. The men who gathered in Philadelphia during the summer of 1787 were public men—politicians—familiar with the art of compromise. But they were also, by and large, learned men, schooled in political philosophy and theory, who brought similar intellectual traditions with them even as they hailed from different states with different interests. They held well-defined views on republican government, the problems with the Articles of Confederation, and the challenges confronting the young nation. As they began their deliberations it became apparent almost immediately that it would not be enough to revise the defective Articles. And so a new national government was proposed. Trying to define the allocation of governing authority between this new national government and those of the several states emerged as a central issue in their deliberations. And it was driven in large part by politics—the push and pull of regional and sectional interests played out among the delegates. Drawing that line between state and national power was what the Constitutional Convention was all about.

THE CONSTITUTIONAL CONVENTION

The formal call for a convention to consider revisions to the Articles of Confederation was issued in September 1786 from representatives of several states meeting in Annapolis. The purpose of that meeting had been to consider ways to deal more effectively with interstate quarrels related to trade, commerce, and transportation. The Philadelphia meeting had taken on the appearance of substantial importance, however, because many of the more prominent individuals involved in public affairs had agreed to attend, most notably George Washington.

Almost from the start of the convention in May 1787, the delegates seemed to form two loose coalitions. On the one side, there were those who recognized the problems inherent in the weak Articles of Confederation but who remained wary of any major reforms that might undermine the political authority of the states. George Mason of Virginia, Elbridge Gerry of Massachusetts, and Roger Sherman of Connecticut could be counted in this camp. On the other hand, there were those who likewise saw the flaws in the Articles but therefore favored fundamental reform and the creation of a new national government with authority to act independent of the states. This was truly a radical proposition that seemed beyond the jurisdiction of the Convention. It had been convened, after all, to revise the Articles, not to replace them. Moreover, as delegates representing their states, any attempt to create a new national government would seem at odds with their very presence in Philadelphia. As delegates, they were pledged to represent the interests of their states; while some delegates had broader instructions, advancing the argument for a new national government seems counter to their assignment. James Madison and Edmund Randolph of Virginia, James Wilson of Pennsylvania, and Alexander Hamilton of New York formed the leadership of this coalition. For that entire summer, the debate transpired between these two groups.

Early into the proceedings, Edmund Randolph, working with James Madison, offered what is now called the Virginia Plan. Madison's strategy was to establish the terms of the debate from the start by having the delegates react to his proposal. He contended that although all in attendance were in agreement about the problems with the Articles of Confederation, few seemed to recognize the real problem. It wasn't that the Articles were a weak confederation; indeed, the Articles created a relatively strong confederation of states. The problem was that no confederation would be adequate to the task at hand. What was needed was a truly national government:

> Resolved that a Union of the States merely federal will not accomplish the objects proposed by the articles of confederation, namely common defense, security of liberty, and general welfare and that a national Government ought to be established consisting of a supreme Legislative, Executive and Judiciary.

Randolph's suggestion was accepted almost immediately as a way of commencing deliberations. It became the blueprint from which the delegates worked for the remainder of the Convention and for the new constitution that would emerge from it. During that hot summer the delegates would turn to it time and again, tinkering with all the various provisions and making many changes. But they never really backed away from the assumption that a supreme national authority was needed. Madison's strategy worked. By getting a proposal for a national government before his colleagues early in the deliberations he framed the subsequent discussions, making it difficult for the defenders of the Articles to press their argument. Those who had journeyed to Philadelphia anxious about the future of the Confederation and of their states found themselves on the defensive almost immediately, therefore, and spent most of their time trying to make sure the new constitution would contain some language guaranteeing the sovereignty of the states and limiting the powers of the new national government. They sought, in other words, to secure a truly federal constitution.

Although the many problems that plagued the Articles seemed evidence enough of the need for fundamental change—the ongoing problems surrounding commerce and taxation and of the privileges and immunities among the states, and the difficulty of making important national policy without unanimity—the fact of the matter was that for most of the delegates history, experience, and political theory provided powerful support for maintaining a decentralized political system in which state governments remained authoritative. They also knew that classic regime theory argued that republican government was possible only when government was small and close to the body of self-governing citizens.

History taught that republics, in order to survive, depend upon the cultivation of civic virtue among the citizens. This can only take place when citizens participate in government, watch over it, and recognize they have a stake in the decisions government makes. The relationship between the citizen and his state has a salutary effect upon both. Republics nurture citizenship and are nurtured by good citizens. Republics are governed by citizens just as they govern those citizens. In theory, a republic keeps government in its place, protects individual liberty, and instills a sense of civic responsibility among the people.

For these reasons, the states seemed the more appropriate locus for government authority. Only by maintaining the sovereignty of the states could republican government flourish. Moreover, the people identified with their states. They were Virginians and Pennsylvanians. The idea of a national identity seemed artificial and distant. Creating a central national government, in other words, not only seemed to pose a threat to the states, it seemed at odds with the idea of classical republicanism.

Madison turned the argument on its head, however, with his defense of the proposed constitution that was published after the Convention in the newspapers of New York. In *The Federalist* No. 10, Madison asserted that there are real problems with small republics—problems related to the tyranny of public opinion that were quite obvious under the Articles of Confederation—and that the only way to deal effectively with those problems was through a large, extensive republic. Madison's discussion of factions and the problems of public opinion in a democracy provided the groundwork for his overall defense of a union of the states and a national government. More important, he mounted an argument that appealed to both experience and principle, thereby undermining the constitution's opponents. It was possible, Madison argued, to have both large size and republican government; indeed, it was preferable.

A large, extended republic would embrace a "multiplicity of interests" making it less likely that an interest "adverse to the rights of other citizens, or to the permanent and aggregate interests of the community" could prevail. Through representative government, Madison reasoned, the republican principle could be in place over a large territory. Representatives chosen by the people would "refine and enlarge the public views." The people choosing their representatives would promote good citizenship. Elections would ensure government was kept in its place. Having a legislative body would limit the tyranny of public opinion. And a large republic offered another advantage: greater security against foreign attacks.

Throughout the summer, those delegates who were leery of a national government pressed for checks on such a government, as well as adequate representation of the states in that government. The resulting compromises are such that, as Madison wrote in *The Federalist Papers*, all three branches of the new national government might rightly be considered "partly national and partly federal." The Congress is composed of a House of Representatives elected directly by the people and should be considered a national institution. The Senate, with its members chosen by state legislatures and with each state having equal representation in the chamber, was a "constitutional recognition of the portion of sovereignty remaining in the individual states, and an instrument for preserving that residual sovereignty." The executive branch is national, but the unique way the President is chosen, through an electoral college by the states, is federal. The judiciary is national and federal: appointed by the President and confirmed by the Senate. The process for amending the Constitution is federal. By September, as the debates drew to their conclusion, most of the delegates remaining felt relatively comfortable with the document, if not completely confident in it.

We forget just how exceptional federalism was at the time. The fact that the Framers chose to "get it down in writing" is significant in and of itself. A written constitution, outlining the authority of government, not only empowers the government but limits it. Moreover, the structure of government created by the Constitution was designed to limit it still further. Separation of powers and checks and balances serve to keep the three branches of the national government in check, so that no single branch can gain too much advantage over the other. By setting "ambition against ambition," as it says in *Federalist* No. 10, the Constitution forces each institution of the national government to work with the other, thereby limiting the exercise of power. The Constitution was designed to get in the way of government and the policymaking process; it was designed to limit government and to make it difficult to make public policy.

Likewise, federalism was thought to limit the national government even more by providing yet another check on it. Whereas separation of powers and checks and balances might be considered a limitation on government across the government's institutions— executive, legislative, and judicial—federalism created a tension between the national and state governments that would keep national power in check as states seek to assert their own authority. Thus, while federalism is not explicitly discussed or defined in the Constitution, it is one of the primarily auxiliary precautions that go beyond the words of the text to give added protections against both majority faction and government tyranny.

The delegates who agreed to send the proposed Constitution to the states for ratification feared that opposition to it would grow as knowledge of it increased. Everyone understood ratification would be a struggle, that it was not a sure thing. During that struggle, no issue so occupied the defenders and opponents of the new Constitution as much as defining what federalism meant. For federalism would define what power this new national government would wield.

Alexander Hamilton, the ardent nationalist, wrote in *The Federalist Papers* that "the task of marking the proper line of partition between the authority of the general and that of the State government" was an arduous one. He sought to persuade his readers that the answer could be found in the text of the Constitution and the principle that states mattered. He was convinced that "two sovereignties cannot coexist with the same limits," and reasoned that this did not imply that the states could not exercise authority independent of the national government. At the New York ratification convention Hamilton said the notion that "two supreme powers cannot act together is false. They are inconsistent only when they are aimed...at one indivisible goal." Hamilton's point was that states and the central government were quite sovereign in their specific spheres of governing responsibility. This was the very point of the compromise that had led to the Constitution. Moreover, Hamilton argued, the citizens, who felt deep loyalty to their states, wanted it that way:

> The early connections we have formed, the habit and prejudices in which we have been bred, fix our affections so strongly that no future objects of association can easily eradicate them.

Hamilton's point, then, was that popular loyalty to the states would both ensure their ongoing vitality and protect against a national government growing too strong and reaching beyond its proper scope of responsibility. The Constitution outlined the powers of the national government, limitations on the national government, and limitations on the powers of the states. Politics would shape how those limitations—how the relationship among governments—developed going forward. And Hamilton would have those who remained wary of the new national government bear some responsibility for keeping it in its place, even as he would become an advocate for expansive national power. In the ensuing years, Hamilton would become the primary architect of a strong, consolidated national government, making many of the arguments he advanced to ensure the political interests of the states ring hollow.

James Madison, who would later go on with Thomas Jefferson to counter many of Hamilton's nationalist positions, mounted a similar argument. Writing in *The Federalist*, he argued that the states retained an important hold over the sentiments of the people and the lion's share of the powers of government under the new Constitution. According to Madison, "The State governments will have the advantages of the federal government" primarily because the national government will be dependent upon the states and the citizens will in all probability side with the states in any dispute between the states and the central government. "The State governments may be regarded as constituent and essential parts of the federal government; whilst the latter is nowise essential to the operation or organization of the former." Madison went on to insist that "each of the principal branches of the federal government will owe its existence more or less to the favor of State governments."

Pennsylvania's James Wilson made much the same argument during his state's ratification convention. For Wilson, federalism meant the states and the central government could exist in harmony together, each exercising authority independent of the other.

> Are disputes between the general government and the state governments to be necessarily the consequences of inaccuracy? I hope, sir, they will not be enemies of each other, or resemble comets in conflicting orbits, mutually operating destruction; but that their motion will be better represented by that of the planetary system, where each part moves harmoniously within its proper sphere, and no injury arises by inference or opposition.

But it was Madison who provided the most direct analysis of the "sphere of responsibility" allocated to each government. Drawing the line between the state and central authority would indeed be difficult, he acknowledged, but that did not mean a line could not be drawn. In *Federalist* No. 45, he drew it:

> The powers delegated by the proposed Constitution to the federal government are few and defined. Those which are to remain in the State governments are numerous and indefinite. The former will be exercised principally on external objects, as war, peace, negotiation, and foreign commerce; with which last the power of taxation will, for the most

part, be connected. The powers reserved to the several States will extend to all the objects which, in the ordinary course of affairs, concern the lives, liberties, and properties of the people, and the internal order, improvement, and prosperity of the States.

The idea of federalism is woven throughout the Constitution. Federalism, as created by the Framers and incorporated into the Constitution, may rightly be considered the fundamental principle underwriting what the *Federalist* calls an "improved science of politics." It set forth the proposition that state sovereignty mattered and should be protected while recognizing the democratic principle that citizens must govern—at the state and national level. It held out the proposition that the nation would benefit from an energetic but limited national government while simultaneously nurturing and being nurtured by sovereign, politically vital states and communities. It carried the promise, as Alexis de Tocqueville observed years later, that America could benefit from the advantages of both large and small size: a great nation with a competent national government that could meet the threats of other nations, and yet a nation where states matter and citizenship is nurtured by political participation at the state and local level. A nation of states.

THE BILL OF RIGHTS

The debate over the ratification of the Constitution was all about how to organize government to ensure the competent exercise of authority while safeguarding the liberties of the people. The compromise concerning the states that was conceived in Philadelphia—federalism—represented a new, novel approach to deal with the old problems of politics in a new age. Nevertheless, the Framers knew that parchment barriers by themselves would settle nothing.

The ratification of the Constitution, while ending the era of the Articles of Confederation, signaled the beginning of a debate that continues to this day on what the Constitution means, how government functions, and how individual liberties are to be protected. It is a debate that has engaged all three branches of the national government, the states, and the citizens themselves. It is a debate that has led to contests and compromises, led a nation into civil war and out of a great depression. In the end, however, just as it has fallen to the courts to "say what the law is," so it has fallen to the federal judiciary to determine, by and large, the contours of government in America and the scope of individual liberty protected by the Constitution.

It might rightly be argued that the debate over the authority of the proposed national government vis-à-vis that of the states gave birth to the Bill of Rights. Put another way, the creation of the Bill of Rights bolsters the argument for federalism. When the Constitution emerged from Philadelphia in 1787, it contained no bill of rights. George Mason of Virginia had raised this oversight toward the end of the Convention, asserting that a listing of rights might be needed to ensure that the new government posed no threat to the citizens of the several states. But his proposal was rejected by his fellow delegates, and the Constitution was sent to the states without a bill of rights.

Two of the leading lights of the Convention, James Madison of Virginia and James Wilson of Pennsylvania, saw no need for a bill of rights. Madison, writing in the newspapers of New York during the ratification debates asserted a bill of rights was superfluous to good government. "Is a bill of rights essential to liberty?" he asked. "The Confederation has no bill of rights." He had a point: How could opposition to the new Constitution be premised on its lacking a bill of rights when the existing Articles contained no such thing? Moreover, the constitutions of the states contained provisions protecting the rights of their citizens. A national bill of rights would be redundant, especially given the argument that the new national government was one of limited, enumerated powers.

But the call for a bill of rights resounded during the ratification debates. Despite persuasive arguments opposing a bill of rights, it became perhaps the single most resonant concern about the Constitution. In many state ratification conventions there was talk of "conditional ratification": approving the Constitution on the condition that it would be amended. Others responded that a conditional ratification was insufficient and argued for withholding approval until changes were made to the document. Still others argued that amendments were premature and that the new constitution needed to be implemented and given time to work before changes to it were appropriately considered. Various versions of amendments were drafted and debated. The issue would not go away.

While the Constitution was ratified, there was less than a general consensus of support for the new government it created. Those who were elected to the First Congress meeting in New York in 1789 knew this. Among its members was James Madison. On June 8 of that year, Madison offered a series of revisions to the Constitution, hoping they would satisfy those who seemed leery of the document while not offending its supporters. Writing to his good friend Thomas Jefferson, Madison remarked, "A bill of rights, incorporated in the constitution will be proposed, with a few other alterations most called for by the opponents of the Government and least objectionable to its friends."

How Madison, a vocal opponent of a bill of rights, came to become its chief sponsor in the House of Representatives is a testimony to the influence of politics on statesmanship. Madison had sought a seat in the U.S. Senate, but the Virginia legislature denied it to him, in large part at the behest of Patrick Henry, a vocal critic of Madison and of the Constitution. Madison then sought election to the House of Representatives. Hoping to defeat him in this as well, Henry persuaded Madison's friend James Monroe to stand for the same seat. Madison hated campaigning, yet, in a deft campaign maneuver, he decided to announce a change of attitude on the need for a bill of rights as a means of "satisfying the minds of the well-meaning opponents, and of providing additional guards in favor of liberty." He now favored "provisions for all essential rights, particularly the rights of Conscience in the fullest latitude, the freedom of the press, trials by jury, security against general warrants etc."

What Madison proposed during the First Congress were revisions to the Constitution that were to be incorporated into the document, not appended to it. The language referencing rights would have been inserted into Article I of the Constitution, that article which pertains to the powers of Congress. It made sense, he reasoned, to list any limitations on the powers of Congress where the powers are enumerated in the document. He also recommended an explicit limitation on the powers of the state governments as well, seeking to incorporate into the Constitution the following: "No State shall violate the equal rights of conscience, of the freedom of the press, or trial by jury in criminal cases."

Madison's proposal failed to arouse much debate and was sent to a committee, where it languished. Eventually many of the recommendations were adopted by the House and sent to the Senate. There changes were made to the format and wording of the revisions. What emerged from the conference between the two chambers were twelve amendments to be added to the Constitution rather than incorporated into the document. Those were then sent to the states for ratification. Ten of the twelve were ratified and became the Bill of Rights in 1791.

Of particular significance for federalism is the fact that Madison's proposal to include language securing rights against state action went nowhere. The Bill of Rights, as finally adopted by Congress and ratified by the states, was an assertion of rights protected against national action, specifically by Congress. This is important. The Bill of Rights was understood by those who drafted and ratified it to be a way of securing individual rights from infringement by the new national government. The First Amendment says "Congress shall make no law . . . ." Moreover, the Bill of Rights was also understood as a protection for the states against encroachments by the national government. State governments were not bound by these provisions. Indeed, most states already had their own bills of rights, and so for protections against state actions individuals looked to their state's constitution. The Bill of Rights was as much a protection of the sovereignty of the states as it was an assurance that certain rights would be safe from national attack.

This comes across quite clearly in the Constitution's Tenth Amendment. Originally, it was Madison's ninth proposition: "The powers not delegated by the constitution, nor prohibited by it to the States, are reserved to the States respectively." Thomas Tucker of South Carolina responded that Madison's proposal should be altered by adding as a prefix "all powers being derived from the people" and inserting "expressly" so that the provision read "the powers not expressly delegated by the constitution." Madison objected, arguing that it was impossible and imprudent to attempt to confine the general government to the exercise of express powers only and equally necessary to allow for powers of implication. Tucker rose to defend his case, but was defeated. Only days later, Elbridge Gerry offered the same proposal, which was also defeated.

The exchange between Madison and Tucker sheds some light on what the eventual Tenth Amendment meant to those who proposed it. According to Madison, the central government was indeed one of limited and enumerated powers. But because it was impossible to define precisely the full scope of the powers enumerated in the Constitution, it was dangerous to use the term "expressly." Madison was making a distinction, therefore, between a government of delegated powers and a government of expressly delegated powers. Both sorts of governments would be limited, for sure. But the latter would be far more limited than the former. The Tenth Amendment recognized the new national government to be a government of delegated powers.

This distinction would give rise to the debate over "implied powers" within the context of limited government, under constitutional language such as "necessary and proper" or "general welfare."

In many ways, the Bill of Rights was the political price the supporters of the new Constitution had to pay its opponents in order to ensure the document survived. It was, after all, the Anti-Federalists who had called for a bill of rights. And it was their concern with limiting the power of the new national government that was embodied in the Tenth Amendment. As Chief Justice Harlan Stone stated years later, the amendment was intended "to allay the fears that the new national government might seek to exercise powers not granted, and that the states might not be able to exercise fully their reserved powers." It states in bold terms the fundamental demarcation of governing power that was at the very center of the debate over the Constitution.

Perhaps the most forceful articulation of the importance of the Bill of Rights to the principle of federalism was uttered only a few years later by none other than Chief Justice John Marshall. Writing for the Court in *Barron v. Baltimore* (1833), Marshall dismissed a plaintiff's case which argued that the Fifth Amendment provision prohibiting the taking of private property for public use without just compensation also restrains state action. After reviewing the provisions in the Constitution that outline the powers of and restraints on the Congress and the states, Marshall saw little to support the plaintiff's contention: "Had the framers of these amendments intended them to be limitations on the powers of the States' governments they would have imitated the framers of the original Constitution, and have expressed their intention." He found further evidence for this position by drawing upon the debates that surrounded the ratification of the Constitution. "In almost every convention by which the Constitution was adopted," Marshall opined, "amendments were recommended. These amendments demanded security against the apprehended encroachments of the general government—not against those of the local governments."

Marshall's opinion takes on greater meaning with regard to federalism, given his nationalist leanings and the earlier decisions the Court had rendered (to be discussed later) regarding the division of authority between the national and state government. With *Barron*, the Court unequivocally supports the Bill of Rights as a protection of state action every bit as much as a prohibition against national action. It is a view very much at odds with the contemporary understanding of the Bill of Rights. But Marshall's view of the applicability of the guarantees in the Bill of Rights held sway for several generations—well into the middle of the 19th century. A war and changes to the Constitution combined with the changing nature of the judiciary to produce a fundamentally different view of the Bill of Rights.

A FUNDAMENTAL PRINCIPLE

What emerged from the summer of 1787 in Philadelphia, and the debates that followed, is an argument about form and scope. Initially, the opponents and supporters of the new government differed about the feasibility of a system of government in which sovereignty is divided among governments. What would such a system of shared or dual sovereignty look like? How could such as system work? A second and more important debate—and one that continues today—concerned how to divide powers among governments. Having established the principle of dual sovereignty, defining the limits of sovereignty for the national and state governments became the ongoing and primary focus of attention. It was a debate about putting principles into practice. And it was resolved, for the moment, by referring to the government created by the Constitution as a limited government of enumerated powers only; as Madison put it, a government whose powers are "few and defined." This argument, coupled with the fact that the populace recognized the deficiencies of the Articles of Confederation, was enough to attract the support needed to ratify the Constitution. But the opponents of the Constitution continued to press their case even after ratification, arguing that it was necessary to clarify the limited nature of the national government and secure the "liberties" of the states.

While the proponents of the new Constitution—the Federalists—prevailed in the struggle over ratification, history suggests the Anti-Federalists might have had the keener insight. Many of the predictions they expressed from the beginning have come to pass. The national government has evolved to exceed many times over the powers enumerated in the Constitution. Over time, the sovereignty of the states has dwindled, challenged time and again by ever-expanding notions of national executive, legislative, and judicial power. But the critics of the Constitution were at a disadvantage from the start; they were less organized and seen as defenders of the flawed Articles rather than advocates of classic republican principles of government. They were victims, as well, of some rhetorical sleight of hand on the part of the Constitution's defenders.

During the 18th century, it was understood that governments were organized around either of two principles. On the one hand, there were unitary or consolidated or centralized or national government, such as the monarchies of Europe. On the other hand, there were decentralized or confederal or federal governments, such as the Swiss Cantons. In other words, when statesmen spoke of governmental organizations or systems, they spoke of either a centralized, consolidated government or a federal or confederal government. Federation and confederation meant the same thing. The idea of some hybrid or combination of a federal and centralized government was unheard of at the time. What quickly acquired the nomenclature of "federalism" was invented with the

American Constitution. And the nomenclature mattered. When the supporters of the Constitution styled themselves as Federalists, they seemed to their countrymen to be both defenders of decentralized government and a new national government at the same time. Labeled Anti-Federalists, the Constitution's opponents might seem to many as opposed to the Articles of Confederation as well as the Constitution, even while they argued for the states. The fact that the new national government quickly acquired the label of "federal" government" suggests just how effective the Federalists were in their advocacy.

Years later, writing in *Democracy in America*, Alexis de Tocqueville picked up on the strategy that had been so skillfully employed by the advocates for the new national government:

> The human understanding more easily invents new things than new words, and we are hence constrained to employ many improper and inadequate expressions. When several nations form a permanent league and establish a supreme authority, which, although it cannot act upon private individuals like a national government, still acts upon each of the confederate states in a body, this government, which is so essentially different from all others, is called Federal. *Another form of society* is afterwards discovered in which several states are fused into one with regard to certain common interests, although they remain distinct, or only confederate, with regard to all other concerns. In this case the central power acts directly on the governed, whom it rules and judges in the same manner as a national government, but in a limited circle. *Evidently this is no longer a federal government, but an incomplete national government, which is neither exactly national nor exactly federal,* but the new word which ought to express this novel things does not yet exist. [Emphasis added]

The principle of federalism that was given birth at the Constitutional Convention and set forth in the Constitution was one of the major themes that informed deliberations during the formative years of the Republic. The whole concept of dual sovereignty was a preoccupation in public affairs. Determining the geography of state and national sovereignty became the principal task of governing. This, in turn, led to the large, still ongoing debate over the notion of limited government, the central tenet of republicanism and one of the animating sentiments behind the idea of having a written constitution.

Chapter 3

Federalism and the Early Republic

T ime has a way of rewriting history. Years go by and facts become forgotten or distorted, and the context in which events unfold becomes lost in the mists of memory. Aggravating all of this is the work of "historians" who seek to "reinterpret" history unencumbered by any knowledge of or appreciation for what actually might have taken place. Given all of this, it is of little surprise that most Americans know little or nothing about the idea of federalism and exhibit a stunning ignorance of American history generally.

The history of federalism is particularly susceptible to distortion due to the fact that many of the nation's most difficult challenges seem related, at least in part, to debates over national versus state authority. The most obvious of these was the Civil War. But from the earliest years of the Republic, controversies over delineating the line of authority between the states and the national government shaped much of the history of the nation and defined much of its politics.

FEDERALISM'S FIRST TESTS

The first test of the power of the new national government created by the Constitution came from a group of farmers on the western frontier of Pennsylvania. In 1790, Congress established a direct tax on whiskey as a part of its new program to raise revenues. The fact that Congress levied a tax on anything was greeted by some with suspicion, given a revolution had been fought against England for just such a reason. But the new government needed funds desperately, and had been created, in part, because the system of government under the Articles of Confederation had possessed no authority to manage money at all. This particular tax, however, encountered the ire of farmers in the frontier regions of the middle and southern states because they sold their surplus grain to whiskey manufacturers. Moreover, a majority of westerners had opposed the adoption of the Constitution and now felt more than put upon that the government would target them for taxation. Political protests gradually became more organized, with meetings held and threats to block execution of the law issued.

Congress, hearing of the protests and eager to assert the authority of the new national government, passed a law in 1792 authorizing the President to call out the militia in case an insurrection occurred against the national authority or in the case that a state, threatened by internal disorder it could not control, asked for help from the national government. The law itself was explicit, however, about ensuring such action should only be a last resort, after any and all civil and governmental procedures had failed. In addition, it required the President to issue a proclamation warning any rebels to disperse before calling out the militia. At about the same time, Congress sought to temper the frustration and anger on the western frontier by lowering the whiskey tax somewhat.

Things continued to heat up. Arguing the tax was robbing them of their property and the right to make a decent living, some seven thousand western Pennsylvanians marched on Pittsburgh in 1794 to try to put an end to the tax. Congress reacted with alarm: "Every honest Citizen must feel himself personally mortified at the conduct of the rioters which, particularly if it passes with impunity, is calculated to fix an indelible stigma on the honor and reputation of the state." President Washington issued his proclamation a few days later, commanding the insurgents in the name of the rule of law to submit to the legitimate national authority. They refused, and the President called for 13,000 militiamen under his command to march west to put down the unrest. The rebellion quickly disintegrated. Some of the leaders were arrested and tried for treason; two were convicted but later pardoned by Washington.

The Whiskey Rebellion is notable for the fact that it represented the first attempt by the national government to enforce an unpopular law through military action upon citizens of the United States. Moreover, it was the first time a President of the United States exercised his explicit authority as commander in chief. Washington personally led the troops; no President has done that since. Most importantly, it established the fact that the new national government possessed the power to enforce its authority.

The Whiskey Rebellion was about citizens protesting a tax. But it took place against a larger backdrop of rising popular and political anxieties about just how powerful this national government might become and how much of that power would come at the expense of the states. The debate that had transpired during the ratification struggle continued, therefore, now within Congress, within the executive branch, and among the citizens generally. While the Federalists controlled Congress, there were not a few members who questioned where things might go, among them James Madison. And while Washington was a committed nationalist, as was his Secretary of the Treasury and close advisor, Alexander Hamilton, his Cabinet included Thomas Jefferson, who openly challenged Hamilton time and again. (Thus establishing the practice of members of a President's administration publicly bickering with one another.) Indeed, the ongoing quarrel between Hamilton and Jefferson was played out in the newspapers at the time in the Federalists' *The Gazette of the United States* and Jefferson's response to it, *The National Gazette*. Jefferson departed Washington's Cabinet in December of 1793, before the President challenged the rebellious frontiersmen in Pennsylvania, and returned to his home in Virginia. From there, he became more visibly and actively engaged in challenging the Federalists, and Hamilton in particular.

Washington himself chose, in 1796, to announce his decision to leave office upon the completion of his second term. His Farewell Address, published first in Philadelphia and then in newspapers everywhere, urged his fellow countrymen to embrace the Union and to reject regional and sectional rivalries. Obviously aware of and moved by the growing spirit of partisanship being spurred on by Jefferson and Hamilton, Washington sought to remind Americans to "properly estimate the immense value" of the Union to their "collective and individual happiness...." He referred to it as the "Palladium" of the safety and prosperity of the people, and urged them to exhibit a love of country and patriotism above and beyond local interests.

> Citizens by birth or choice, of a common country, that country has a right to concentrate your affections. The name of AMERICAN, which belongs to you, in your national capacity, must always exalt the just pride of Patriotism, more than any appellation derived from local discriminations.

In his Farewell, Washington asserted that it also made sense for Americans to embrace the new nation because they stood to benefit individually and together more from collaboration among regions than from rivalry, and as a Union the strength of the nation provided security against "external danger." He warned of the "Spirit of Party" and against passionate attachments to or hatreds of foreign countries. And he urged the nation to "steer clear of permanent Alliances with any portion of the foreign world."

The first President's warnings were widely read, and his Address has become one of the fundamental documents of American history. But even as the words were written, the growing "spirit of party" was fueling a national debate over what direction the young nation should take.

THE GROWING PARTY DIVIDE

In the first contested election for President, in 1796, the Federalists chose Washington's vice president, John Adams. The nascent Republicans selected Thomas Jefferson. Both parties appealed directly to the citizens through rallies, handbills, and posters. Both parties drew much of their support from different regions and interests: the Republicans from the South and backcountry, small merchants, small farmers, and tradesmen; the Federalists from New England and the Atlantic seaports, commercial, manufacturing, and banking interests. These two broad and loose coalitions, then, formed the outlines of the emerging two-party system in American politics. The names of the parties have changed over time, as have the coalitions that support them and the issues that drive the partisanship. But in 1796, a central issue was the scope of national power and the potential threat it represented to the states. The character of the national government—how it operates, what it does, and how it does it—has, from the beginning, then, been a central theme in American partisan politics. Adams won the election to replace Washington, receiving three more electoral votes than Jefferson, who became vice president. The Federalists retained control of Congress.

The election of 1796 reflected, as well, partisan division in the United States over the war between England and France that had commenced in 1793. The Federalists generally supported Great Britain, looking to the French Reign of Terror as evidence of the folly of empowering unschooled and unpropertied "democrats." Self-styled Republicans, followers of Jefferson and James Madison, hailed the advent of a democratic republic in France and the "leveling" influence more democracy and popular sovereignty would bring to America. This spilled into fierce political rhetoric and Republican criticism of the Adams Administration after the election. An undeclared naval "war" with France raised the level of rhetoric even more. And this prompted the Federalist Congress to seek to quiet the criticism.

The Alien and Sedition Acts, four laws passed in 1798, were aimed at suppressing political opposition and quelling support for France. The Alien Act gave the President the power to imprison or deport foreigners believed to be dangerous to the United States; it was never enforced. The Sedition Act made it a crime to attack the government of the United States through "false, scandalous, or malicious" statements. In effect, it became a crime to criticize the government. Republicans saw the Sedition Act for what it was: an attempt to shut them up. Indeed, approximately 25 Republican newspaper editors and publishers were prosecuted under the Act, and ten were convicted.

Republican hopes that a judge would find the Sedition Act unconstitutional were dashed. They saw it as invading individual rights and state sovereignty. There was loose talk, led by John Taylor of Virginia, of his and other states seceding. Jefferson saw that as too dangerous to countenance and sought other ways to convince his fellow citizens that the Act should not stand. Covertly working with James Madison (Jefferson was, after all, vice president in a Federalist Administration), he saw to it that drafts of resolutions denouncing the law were introduced in the state legislatures of Virginia and Kentucky. Jefferson wrote the draft of the Kentucky Resolution himself; Madison drafted the Virginia Resolution. He reasoned that the prestige enjoyed by state legislatures would make it difficult for the Congress or the judiciary to ignore popular contempt for the Act. It was an attempt to rally the states against the law and to force the Federalists to get rid of it.

The two resolutions were powerful statements about the authority of states to make judgments and take action concerning the constitutionality of national acts. While the Virginia Resolution expressed "a warm attachment to the union of the states," it went on to assert that the states were parties to a "compact" that created the national government under the Constitution and that when that government exercised powers "not granted by said compact" the states have a "right" and are "duty bound" to assert their authority "for arresting the progress of the evil, and for maintaining within their respective limits the authorities, rights, and liberties appertaining to them." The Kentucky Resolution went even further. It asserted that the national government, created by a constitutional compact, "was not made the exclusive or final judge of the extent of the powers delegated to itself." Indeed, each state "has an equal right to judge for itself, as well of infractions as of the mode and measure of redress." And, according to the resolution, the Sedition Law was "altogether void and of no force" in Kentucky. It asserted that the states would not easily submit to congressional actions deemed beyond their constitutional authority and ended with the bold proposition that "these and successive acts of the same character, unless arrested on the threshold, may tend to drive these States into revolution and blood." Jefferson's original draft of the Kentucky Resolution contained language that would reappear years later as the controversy over slavery and state sovereignty spilled into civil war: "where powers are assumed which have not been delegated, a nullification of the act is the right remedy."

The Virginia and Kentucky Resolutions asserted important arguments about the nature of the Constitution and the appropriate exercise of power under it. They framed the Constitution as a compact among the states which each individual state signed on to. This being the case, each state retained the authority to determine for itself when that compact has been violated and to act accordingly; this was a direct repudiation of the Judiciary Act of 1789, which established the Supreme Court and the role of the judiciary in settling constitutional questions, later expounded in *Marbury v. Madison*. Moreover, the national government, according to the Resolutions, was limited by "the plain sense and implication" of the Constitution.

Both the Resolutions embraced a theory of constitutional government that lurked in the background for another generation. But Jefferson and Madison were really engaged in a political battle, employing the Resolutions and state legislatures to wage the fight. The national government never responded to the Resolutions, and no other state signed on. Southern state legislatures were closely divided on the issue, and Northern ones were dominated by Federalists who supported the Acts. In the North, legislatures asserted it was the obligation and duty of the courts to judge the constitutionality of congressional actions. But one state, Vermont, spoke directly to the theory of the Union espoused in the Resolutions: "The people of the United States formed the federal constitution, and not the states, or their legislatures." In any event, Congress did not seem cowed by the Resolutions, and neither Virginia nor Kentucky took any actions to prevent enforcement of the Alien and Sedition Acts. In 1800, efforts were made in the House of Representatives to repeal the Sedition Act, but the Senate refused to consent. It expired in 1801.

The primary effect of the Virginia and Kentucky Resolutions was to keep alive the argument that the United States was a union of sovereign states that had a say in shaping the power of the national government. They cast some doubt over just how "sovereign" the national government was. And they laid the groundwork for a bolder assertion of state sovereignty years later when John C. Calhoun defended the authority of states to "nullify" national action during the debates leading up to the Civil War. They were political responses to an assertion of power by the governing Federalist Party and helped to fuel growing support for the Jeffersonian Republicans. And they ensured the debate over the character of American federalism was far from over.

THE MARSHALL COURT

Not surprisingly, the courts have played a major role in the transformation of American federalism. The debate about the scope of state versus national authority was at the center of political and legal discourse almost from the birth of the Constitution in 1787. Initially, the distrust of centralized and consolidated power that was at the core of the American Revolution was a powerful influence in both politics and law. Over time, and with the gradual acceptance of the new Constitution and its national government, this concern with consolidated power ran up against the recognition of the need for a national government. This tension was most apparent during the ratification debates. And the themes from those debates shaped the discussions and the opinions of the Supreme Court during its early, formative years. Justices turned to those debates as authoritative sources for their opinions. But it became the responsibility of the Court to fashion the contours of the "compound Republic" Madison wrote about in *The Federalist*.

It is fair to say that most Americans identified with the states wherein they resided during the early years of the Republic. The idea of an American national identity and character—what others have referred to as an American "creed"—evolved over time. This had an effect upon the Court as it was forced to settle disputes over state and national authority. Moreover, the states were the hubs of political activity and competent in governing the day-to-day affairs of the country. As issues relating to commerce and trade, national defense, and internal improvements emerged, the authority of the national government inescapably came into question. In other words, as the needs and interests of a nation emerged, the ability of states to meet those needs and interests was brought into question.

From the ratification of the Constitution until the Civil War, the Supreme Court seemed to seek a constitutional middle ground as it charted the geography of federalism. In some areas, it bowed to the authority of the states. In others it upheld the powers of the new national government. A sort of "dual federalism" emerged, as the Court sought to outline the powers of the states and Washington rather than prefer one to the other. Chief Justice John

Jay sketched the contours of such thinking in 1790: The Court "provides against Discord between national and State jurisdictions, to render them auxiliary instead of hostile to each other; and to connect both as to leave each sufficiently independent, and yet sufficiently combined."

An early foray into the federalism debate led to an immediate backlash from the states and Congress. In *Chisholm v. Georgia* (1793), the Court ruled it could resolve a dispute between an individual and a state in which that individual did not reside. Clearly at odds with what the Framers of the Constitution had envisioned, Congress reacted quickly to propose what became the Eleventh Amendment: "The judicial power of the United States shall not be construed to extend to any suit in law or equity, commenced or prosecuted against one of the United States by Citizens of another State, or by Citizens or Subjects of any foreign State." But this did not lead to overwhelming reticence on the part of the federal judiciary. In *Martin v. Hunter's Lessee* (1816), the Court found it could review a decision made by a state's highest court pertaining to the federal Constitution or federally enacted statutes. Here Justice Joseph Story dismissed out of hand any argument that the federal courts were limited in their authority to review state decisions. "It is a mistake that the Constitution was not designed to operate upon states, in their corporate capacities." He went on to say:

> The courts of the United States can, without question revise the proceedings of the executive and legislative authorities of the states, and if they are found to be contrary to the Constitution, may declare them to be of no legal validity. Surely the exercise of the same right over judicial tribunals is not a higher or more dangerous act of sovereign power.

There were practical as well as constitutional reasons behind Story's assertion. The need for "uniformity of decisions throughout the whole United States" made the decision almost a practical necessity.

In 1821, the Court upheld the principle that a state "is not suable except by its own consent" while simultaneously asserting that "the general government, though limited as to its objects, is supreme with respect to those objects." *Cohens v. Virginia* (1821). But the first major test of federalism before the Supreme Court came in 1824, and regarded the meaning of the Constitution's Commerce Clause.

In *Gibbons v. Ogden* (1824), the Court was asked to determine what the Commerce Clause meant in a dispute over steamships and steamship licenses to carry travelers between and among states. Daniel Webster, arguing for Gibbons, asserted that the authority of the national government was complete in this area. "The power of Congress to regulate commerce was complete and entire," he argued, and it "was vain to look for precise and exact definition of the power of Congress, on several subjects." His opponent, Thomas Oakley, countered that Congress's authority was limited to those powers expressly granted in the Constitution: "The Constitution of the United States is one of limited and expressly delegated powers, which can only be exercised as granted, or in the cases enumerated." Oakley's position was grounded, he observed, in a larger argument—"the nature of the Constitution itself, as being a delegation of power"—from the states. Moreover, he asserted the Tenth Amendment made that abundantly clear.

Chief Justice John Marshall, in an important decision, took issue with the whole debate over how to interpret the Constitution. "What do gentlemen mean by strict construction?" he asked. For Marshall the issue was really quite straightforward: "The genius and character of the whole government seems to be, that its action is to be applied to all the external concerns of the nation, and to those internal concerns which affect the states generally; but not to those which are completely within a particular state…." For Marshall, then, interstate commerce meant commerce between and among states; and carrying passengers on rivers flowing between two states was commerce and subject to federal regulation.

Marshall had spoken in an earlier case regarding Oakley's argument that the national government was one of limited, delegated powers only. In the landmark *McCullough v. Maryland* (1819), he opined that it "would be difficult to sustain this proposition" that the powers of the national government "are delegated by the states, who alone are truly sovereign." Rather, Marshall wrote, "the government of the Union is ... emphatically, and truly a government of the people" and "though limited in its powers, is supreme within its sphere of action." Referring to the debates in the First Congress over what became the Tenth Amendment, he noted that the amendment omits the word "expressly" and that the Constitution's Necessary and Proper Clause provided for Congress to exercise those powers needed to put its delegated powers into effect. "Let the end be legitimate, let it be within the scope of the Constitution, and all means which are appropriate ... are constitutional."

The dispute, over the ability of the state of Maryland to tax the national bank located within the state, spoke to a number of issues. Just because the Constitution does not expressly say the national government can run a bank does not mean it cannot run a bank as an appropriate exercise of its powers to raise revenues, borrow money, coin money, and in the exercise of its spending powers. Moreover, should Maryland possess the authority to tax a national bank, it would, in the eyes of the Court, have the ability to put it out of existence—"The power to tax involves the power to destroy"—which would undermine the national government's constitutional prerogatives. It was the first in a line of cases that would look to the implied powers of the national government—found in the Necessary and Proper Clause—to expand, in fits and starts, the authority of the national government, and, at times, limit the sovereignty of the states.

These early years in the Republic saw the Court seek to balance a concern with the consolidation of national authority with a due regard for the authority of the states. In *McCullough* the Court began outlining the scope of the Necessary and Proper Clause of the Constitution. This would have obvious implications for the states. But other cases seemed to reflect an ongoing concern by the justices not to undermine the relatively fragile union of the states. And early on it was a relatively fragile union. Threats of dissolution and secession abounded. Moreover, people identified with their home state far more than with the new national government. The Court understood this. So, while it held that states cannot violate the Contracts Clause of the Constitution, it also deferred to states regarding their internal policies and improvements. It held that the Commerce Clause could be understood to provide a uniform or national regulation among states but also to be respectful of the authority of states to regulate commerce within their borders.

Chapter 4

A Nation Divided

The next major manifestation of the changing nature of federalism, and the true test of the Union, came at mid-century with the United States Civil War. The philosophical seeds of that war were sown much earlier.

On June 2, 1788, Patrick Henry stood before his fellow delegates assembled in Richmond, Virginia, to debate the proposed constitution. Clearly agitated, the renowned orator asked the fundamental question that would drive the Union, years later, to civil war. Citing the "worthy characters" who composed the "federal Convention," Henry had no doubts that "they were fully impressed with the necessity of forming a consolidated government." But he questioned where they got the authority to do such a thing:

> I have the highest veneration for those gentlemen; but, sir, give me leave to demand, What right had they to say *We, the people?* My political curiosity, exclusive of my anxious solicitude for the public welfare, leads me to ask, Who authorized them to speak the language of, *We, the people*, instead of, *We, the states?*

Virginia, of course, went on to vote to ratify the Constitution—over Henry's strong objections. But his question resonated with many and provided, in a way, some rationale for the Virginia and

Kentucky Resolutions that appeared during the Adams Administration and for the theory of nullification that was given full effect by John C. Calhoun in the early 1800s. Calhoun's argument was foreshadowed, as well, by actions taken by a group of New England states protesting the War of 1812.

President Jefferson's anti-foreign-trade policies, enacted in 1807 and 1809, had been very unpopular in the New England states. Jefferson's successor, James Madison had continued the policies, and his prosecution of the War of 1812 had contributed to the animosity that New Englanders felt toward the national government under the leadership of the Republican Party. So in 1814, the Massachusetts state legislature called for a convention to discuss amending the Constitution to protect New England interests. Meeting in Hartford, delegates from the five New England states issued a report that asserted that New England had a duty to protect its sovereignty against unconstitutional infringements.

The Hartford Convention proposed several changes to the Constitution, all aimed at Republican administration policies. The Convention called for limiting Presidents to one term and requiring future Presidents to be from a different state than their predecessor. It also sought to make it more difficult for Congress to declare war, admit new states to the Union, and limit foreign commerce.

The action of the New England states was born of sectional jealousy as much as partisan rivalry. The proposed amendments sought to diminish the influence of the South and the "Virginia Dynasty" as much as to strike back at the trade and foreign commerce policies embraced by Jefferson and Madison. Moreover, the delegates knew that there was no hope that their proposals would be passed by a Republican Congress. The Convention, then, was an attempt to embarrass the President and to establish New England's political authority. Although no such resolution passed, there was some talk of secession and the formation of an independent republic. Massachusetts did send commissioners to Washington to begin "negotiations," but the end of the War of 1812 settled the matter for the time being.

The actions of the New Englanders did not go unnoticed. The Hartford Convention, and the dying Federalist Party that had supported it, became synonymous with secession and attempts to disrupt the Union. The Federalist Party all but disappeared after the Convention. But the arguments regarding state and sectional authority and interests clashing with the national exercise of governmental and political power continued to mount.

THE NULLIFICATION CRISIS

One person who no doubt followed the Hartford Convention was a young congressman from South Carolina, John Caldwell Calhoun. He, along with Henry Clay, had advocated war with England; he was also a strong defender of Southern interests over those of the North. In 1817, he became President Monroe's secretary of war, and in 1824, vice president to John Quincy Adams. He continued in that role under President Andrew Jackson until a disagreement over trade and tariff issues led him to resign in 1832. That disagreement ran deep and led to Calhoun's assertion of the authority of states to nullify federal laws.

During the Administrations of Monroe, J.Q. Adams, and Jackson, the nation underwent considerable change and some economic hardship. While Monroe had ushered in the so-called Era of Good Feelings, the debate over the authority of the states and the national government continued. Monroe largely sided with the Republicans regarding domestic issues; for instance, he opposed "internal improvements." In international affairs he was willing to be more expansive, issuing his Monroe Doctrine in 1832. But the issue that defined the Monroe Administration was the question of statehood for Missouri. Here a simple but profound constitutional question was posed: Could Congress employ the act of admitting a new state to the Union to prohibit the existence of slavery in that state? The Congress was divided on the question and the debate and impasse lasted for years. Congress engaged in lengthy and emotional exchanges on the morality of slavery, the authority of the states, and the meaning of the Constitution. The Missouri Compromise of 1820, which admitted Missouri into the Union as a slave state but prohibited slavery in the territory north of the new state, served to put off the need to reach final resolution of the issue. Thomas Jefferson, in private correspondence at the time, put the issue into proper perspective: "We have the wolf by the ears, and we can neither hold him, nor safely let him go. Justice is in one scale, and self-preservation in the other."

John Quincy Adams entered office after being elected by the House of Representatives and oversaw a divided nation. Supporters of Andrew Jackson felt the election of 1824 had been stolen and agitated against Adams from the onset. Moreover, Adams embraced an activist agenda for his Administration, proposing various "internal improvements" such as roads and turnpikes, canals, and universities. His ideas were dismissed by Congress and much of the country, albeit many of his proposals came to pass later. But Adams never really had the support of his party or of Congress, and in 1828 he lost to Andrew Jackson.

Jackson ushered in a brand of populist politics and democracy that was new to American politics. He introduced a "policy of rotation"—a spoils system—into the operation of the government, aimed at ending its seeming elitism. He enforced policies that removed American Indians to the lands reserved for them west of the Mississippi River. And he sought to control government expenditures and to eliminate the national debt. It was in this effort that he and Calhoun parted ways.

Prior to Jackson's election, Congress had raised a tariff as high as 50 percent on goods made in Europe. Known widely as the Tariff of Abominations, Southerners saw it as aimed at their region and intended to assist Northern manufacturers. Vice President Calhoun secretly worked in his home state of South Carolina to undermine the tariff, all the while hoping the new President would eliminate it.

The "South Carolina Exposition and Protest," drafted by Calhoun, was presented to the South Carolina House of Representatives in December of 1828. It argued that the Tariff of Abominations was aimed at helping one section of the country to the detriment of another and was, therefore, an improper act not authorized by the Constitution. Calhoun asserted a familiar argument on the nature of constitutional government: "The Government is one of specific powers, and it can rightfully exercise only the powers expressly granted, and those being 'necessary and proper' to carry them into effect; all others being reserved expressly to the States, or to the people." Using words that had been rejected by the Framers of the Constitution and the Tenth Amendment, Calhoun posited the need for an "expressed" grant of authority in the Constitution and that all other powers were "expressly" reserved to the states or the people. The Constitution, he continued, authorizes Congress to lay and collect taxes for the "sole purpose of revenue," which does not include "imposing protective or prohibitory duties." The power of Congress to impose duties on imports, Calhoun argued, "is abused by being converted into an instrument for rearing up the industry of one section of the country on the ruins of another." "The violation then consists in using a power, granted for one object, to advance another, and that by the sacrifice of the original object."

The "Exposition" went on to allege the purposeful sectionalism embraced by the tariff, finding that its "burdens are exclusively on one side and its benefits on the other." The goal, he concluded, was to suppress the South.

> It is then not a subject of wonder, when properly understood, that one section of country though blessed by a kind Providence with a genial sun and prolific soil, from which spring the richest products, should languish in poverty and sink into decay; while

the rest of the Union though less fortunate in natural advantages is flourishing in prosperity beyond example.

After detailing the evidence for this proposition, Calhoun launched into an attack on unchecked majority rule—"an unchecked majority, is a despotism"—and the importance of the Constitution as a check on the majority. But when that check is either ignored or denied, he argued, the states have an obligation to assert their own check.

> With these views the committee are solemnly of the impression if the system be preserved in, after due forbearance on the part of the State, that it will be her sacred duty to interpose her veto; a duty to herself, to the Union, to present, and to future generations, and to the cause of liberty over the world, to arrest the progress of a power, which, if not arrested, must in its consequences, corrupt the public morals, and destroy the liberty of the country.

Calhoun ended the document with an appeal "to the justice and good feeling of those States heretofore opposed to us" and sought the "co-operation of those States, similarly situated with our own." It was an appeal for the South to join hands in defiance of Washington.

The South Carolina House of Representatives never adopted the resolution, choosing instead to wait and see if the incoming President would support or oppose the tariff. But it was widely distributed and read and became the conceptual and philosophical basis for the idea of nullification and the assertion of "states' rights" in the years leading up to the Civil War.

In what must have been a chilly exchange loaded with political implications, Jackson offered his opinion of the issue during a Jefferson Day dinner in April 1830, with Vice President Calhoun in attendance. Jackson toasted to "our union: It must be preserved."

Calhoun then rose to reply: "The Union, next to our liberty, most dear. May we always remember that it can only be preserved by distributing equally the benefits and burdens of the Union." Calhoun soon resigned his office.

But the debate continued and the issue continued to fester. In 1832, eager to calm regional animosities, Jackson proposed a lower tariff. The national debt was gone, after all. But Southerners were not swayed, and the protective principle of the tariff remained in effect. In protest, South Carolina found both the original tariff and the new Jackson tariff to be "null and void," and the legislature voted to raise an army to defend its nullification action. In the face of a clear constitutional crisis, Jackson would not back down. He declared nullification illegal and the Union indissoluble. Asking Congress to authorize him to enforce federal law, the President then sent a fleet of ships to Charleston Harbor. Jackson's Nullification Proclamation, at the time, represented the boldest statement made by a President in defense of national action and the Union. He began his response with an attack on the very idea the ordinance passed by the South Carolina was based on: "The strange proposition that one state may not only declare an Act of Congress void, but prohibit its execution." From here, Jackson went on the attack:

> I consider then the power to annul a law of the United States, assumed by one State, INCOMPATIBLE WITH THE EXISTENCE OF THE UNION, CONTRADICTED EXPRESSLY BY THE LETTER OF THE CONSTITUTION, UNAUTHORIZED BY ITS SPIRIT, INCONSISTENT WITH EVERY PRINCIPLE ON WHICH IT WAS FOUNDED, AND DESTRUCTIVE OF THE GREAT OBJECT FOR WHICH IT WAS FORMED....

The Constitution of the United States, then, forms a government, not a league, and whether it be formed by compact between the States, or in any other manner, its character is the same. It is a government in which all the people are represented, which operates directly on the people individually, not upon the States—they retained all the power they did not grant. But each State having expressly parted with so many powers as to constitute jointly with the other States a single Nation, cannot from that period possess any right to secede, because each secession does not break a league, but destroys the unity of a Nation, and any injury to that unity is not only a breach which would result from the contravention of a compact, but it is an offense against the whole Union....

The laws of the United States must be executed. I have no discretionary power on the subject—my duty is emphatically pronounced in the Constitution. Those who told you that you might peaceably prevent their execution, deceived you—they could not have been deceived themselves. ...Their object is disunion: but be not deceived by names: disunion, by armed force, is TREASON....

South Carolina backed down. With the help of Henry Clay, Jackson approved a tariff with even lower levels of protection. Although no other state signed on to South Carolina's position, that didn't mean the issue was resolved. For while South Carolina was a lone voice: the economic decline that it and much of the South was experiencing caused ongoing anxiety. Calhoun continued to be an advocate of both slavery—he came to argue that slavery was a "positive good"—and state sovereignty until his death in 1850.

SLAVERY AND CIVIL WAR

As economic issues merged with a concern over the future of slavery, fueled by militant abolitionism in the North and rumored and real slave insurrections in the South, the debate over state sovereignty became inextricably linked with the issue of slavery. Sectionalism became fused with pro-slavery and abolitionist sentiments. Tensions continued to rise, and national politics was soon defined by those tensions. In 1857, the Supreme Court contributed to the discord when it handed down its decision in *Dred Scott v. Sanford* (1857). Here the Court had sought to answer a question that had defined much of the bitter politics confronting the nation for years: Could Congress prohibit slavery in the territories? The issue was whether a slave, having resided for years in both a free state and a free territory, was thereby no longer a slave.

Chief Justice Roger Taney spoke for the Court, although each justice wrote a separate opinion. Arguing that, at the time of the writing of the Declaration of Independence and the Constitution, "the class of persons who had been imported as slaves [and] their descendents" were widely regarded as "an inferior order and altogether unfit to associate with the white race," Taney found that Dred Scott was not a citizen of the United States, nor of any state. Hence, he possessed no right to sue in federal court for his freedom. Moreover, Taney held that Congress had no authority to prohibit slavery in a territory. In Taney's opinion, slaves were property. The Constitution's Fifth Amendment prohibits Congress from taking property without due compensation. Taney reasoned, if that limited Congress with regard to the states, it limited Congress with regard to territories as well. Therefore, "neither Dred Scott himself, nor any of his family, were made free by being carried into this territory; even if they had been carried there by the owner with the intention of becoming a permanent resident."

With the Court's opinion, the Missouri Compromise's free state-slave state tradeoff was invalidated, and the nation's political crisis worsened. The next year, Abraham Lincoln of Illinois accepted his party's nomination to run for the Senate and delivered his famous speech declaring "a house divided against itself cannot stand." Although defeated, he would soon acquire a national stature and become President just as the Civil War began to erupt.

The causes and effects of the Civil War are much too numerous to analyze here. Surely slavery, the "wolf by the ear" that had plagued the nation since before its creation, was the singular issue that transformed a debate about the limits of national and state power into a moral cause about the rights of men and women and the power of the national government generally. But with the Civil War the debate ended and the fighting began. In the end, after years of bloody conflict, the nation, while not truly united, was no longer divided. And any debate about federalism and the sovereignty of the states had been quieted—at least for the moment.

Abraham Lincoln understood clearly what was at stake as he entered the presidency: the Constitution. The issue of slavery was surely a moral one. But it was a political issue as well. Lincoln had been willing to put aside his own views about slavery in order to avert a civil war. But with the secession of Southern states and the onset of hostilities, that was no longer necessary. Asserting the act of secession to be at odds with the very nature of the Constitution, he called for 75,000 militiamen to quell the rebellion.

Lincoln's understanding of federalism under the Constitution had little room for state sovereignty, a theory that did not appear in the document, after all. Nor did he give much credence to the idea, advanced by Calhoun and others, of a "compact" between the states and the national government. For Lincoln, the Constitution was perpetual, resting on the consent of "we the people." Moreover, Lincoln argued that the Declaration of Independence had given birth to the United States as a nation and that pure state sovereignty was, by that act of independence and according to the Constitution, non-existent. Secession would turn that on its head by allowing a few states, without the consent of the others, to break the bond of the nation. Prior to the war, he might have been willing to compromise on issues to preserve the Union. With secession, he saw the greater principle to be the preservation of the nation. His concern with "nation" over "union" was reflected in his speeches. Before the Civil War, and in his First Inaugural Address, Lincoln spoke of the importance of the Union. But as the war progressed, he spoke almost always of the nation, seeking to promote a national sentiment which a union had failed to provide.

Lincoln's prosecution of the Civil War, coupled with his strong assertion of national over sectional interests and commitment to equality, transformed the country and the debate over federalism. With the war's end, all talk of secession ceased. But that did not put an end to the larger discussion over state versus national power.

In the aftermath of the Civil War, the Constitution was amended three times. The Thirteenth Amendment abolished slavery, the Fourteenth Amendment's primary purpose was to establish the legal and political rights of the newly freed slaves, and the Fifteenth guaranteed former slaves the right to vote. The Fourteenth Amendment in particular also helped to usher in dramatic changes in how the Constitution would shape the new relationship between the states and the Bill of Rights. The Fourteenth Amendment (adopted in 1868) provides, in part, that "No State shall...abridge the privileges or immunities of citizens of the United States; nor shall any State deprive any person of life, liberty, or property, without due process of law; nor deny to any person within its jurisdiction the equal protection of the laws." As we shall see, the phrases "due process" and "equal protection" would become the opening for the judiciary's modern rights revolution.

It is hard to overstate the impact of the Civil War on the character and conscience of the nation. It was the defining event of the 19th century and immensely influential in the 20th as well. The Constitution was amended after the war in an attempt to put into writing responses to those issues relating to slavery, equality, and citizenship that had ripped the nation apart. But the amendments could not change a culture nor heal past practices nor eradicate ancient habits and prejudices. While the Constitution, with the Fourteenth Amendment, made it impossible to ignore the principle of legal equality, ensuring that "equal protection of the law" has proven difficult. The meaning of the Equal Protection Clause is today a hotly debated question, making the promise of equality one of the great ongoing challenges for our nation.

DO STATES HAVE RIGHTS?

One lingering legacy of the Civil War has been the lasting confusion surrounding the language of federalism. Well into the next century, and still today in some places and at certain times, discussions of federalism have been laced with references to "States' Rights." There is some reason for this, of course. It was the South's embrace of States' Rights that, in the end, propelled the nation into war. But it is useful to wade into this linguistic and political quagmire in order to understand better what distinguishes constitutional federalism from States' Rights.

First things first: States don't have rights. Individuals have rights. Governments, at all levels, have various powers, but not rights. Indeed, the very purpose of the Constitution is to delegate (and withhold) power to government precisely because it is the governed who are sovereign and possess unalienable rights by nature. This is no minor political or philosophical point. To merge federalism with States' Rights too often tends to confuse the meaning of both terms.

As the debate over the sovereignty of the states versus the authority of the national government developed in the early years of the Republic, the attempt to assert state authority took on many forms. With the advancement of the Kentucky and Virginia Resolutions, the ideas of nullification and interposition, and then with secession itself, the rhetoric employed by advocates for the states sought to analogize the plight of the states to that of an individual caught in a contract or compact that he no longer wants to honor. Just as that individual might want to assert a right to break away from the agreement when he feels its terms have been broken by the other party, so might a state want to exercise that "right" when the national government, in its estimation, has violated the compact. As the tensions, and the stakes, grew, so did the heat of the rhetoric. The Southern states, feeling their very survival was being threatened, sought to assert their "right" to defend themselves against the national government every bit as much as an individual might assert such a right against an enemy. States' Rights became a battle cry every bit as much as a political position.

After the Civil War, well into the next century, States' Rights remained the rhetorical device employed by those interested in maintaining the culture, mores, habits, and practices of the segregated South, in spite of changes in law, government, and politics. It was invoked by Southern political leadership eager to protect a segregated society when told by the Supreme Court and then Congress that such a society was at odds with the Constitution. It is still invoked by those whose devotion to a defeated cause and lost way of life overrides any regard for constitutional principle or moral authority. What was once a legitimate argument and rallying cry has come to symbolize the misguided romanticism of a lost cause and at the same time the terrible injustice of a whole slave-based society.

Federalism's roots are much deeper and more profound than States' Rights and stretch back, as we have seen, to the formative years of the Republic. To equate any assertion of state authority as a resort to States' Rights is to cheapen a constitutional principle that was at the very heart of the creation of the Constitution and the nation. The two terms need to be distinguished. The idea of States' Rights should be understood within its historical context. All too often, when the term is employed today it is either in an attempt to appeal to old passions and causes or to conjure up images associated with racism and discrimination. But a resort to States' Rights is rightly understood as an assertion of an important constitutional and political principle. The principle of federalism should be given the prominence and attention intended by the Framers of the Constitution.

THE NEW NATIONALISM

While the Civil War tore the nation apart, the Constitution survived it, amended but intact, as did the national government and an injured but permanent Union. In the years immediately after the war, the relationship of Washington to the states was shaped in the South by reconstruction and, in the North, by the gathering forces of economic development. The war did have a centralizing effect, to be sure. A new national banking system was created. Congress increased national control over the monetary system. Issues of state sovereignty, as they related to secession, were settled. But after the Reconstruction Amendments were ratified, the Congress exhibited a shrinking interest in getting involved in the day-to-day affairs of the Southern states. The Fifteenth Amendment's language provided Congress with the authority to coerce Southern states to grant blacks the vote, but it chose to stop short of getting actively engaged in the determination of the franchise in the South.

As the nation struggled to overcome the hardships of internal war, it turned its attention to economic, industrial, and commercial development and the gradual emergence of the nation as a major economic engine. During the post-war era, America began its transformation from a largely agrarian nation to an industrial one. During the war, the North had increased production of steel, coal, iron, and brass. Now, during America's post-war industrial revolution, economic and commercial development accelerated. Manufacturing exploded, as did railroads, meat packing, lumber, and textiles. By the end of the century, America would be the world's greatest industrial nation.

During this time, the old federalism debates over national and state authority were quieted. Few were interested in returning to a debate that had produced such monumental consequences. But perhaps just as importantly, the nation's focus was on economic growth and development. Ironically, while Congress now possessed authority to become more involved in the affairs of states, through the Fourteenth Amendment, it chose not to do so.

During the industrial revolution, then, the states possessed most of the authority to regulate the growing economic activities taking place within their borders. But interestingly, state legislatures demonstrated a *laissez-faire* attitude, recognizing the growing benefits to be derived by letting the economy grow. Industry was doing well, people were benefiting, and there was widespread hostility toward governmental paternalism.

Just as importantly, business and industry courted state legislators and political leaders to ensure they remained sympathetic to their interests. This began to change in 1887 when Congress passed the Interstate Commerce Act, which established the Interstate Commerce Commission. The goal of the act was to provide the national government with a vehicle to regulate commerce among the states. It was aimed at the railroads, which until then were regulated by and large by the states. Yet while the Commission's scope   initially was limited by the courts, it gradually expanded. The national government got into the business of business a few years later with the passage of the Sherman Anti-Trust Act. The large accumulation of wealth by a relative handful of individuals had produced both the "Gilded Age" and some popular resentments. Congress, concerned about abusive business practices, cartels, and predatory activity, sought a tool to regulate business, and the Sherman Act was a milestone; albeit Washington continued to restrain itself regarding much of the activity going on among the states. Even with the Interstate Commerce Act and the Sherman Anti-Trust Act, states retained oversight of such things as labor laws, family laws, property, criminal justice, and business regulation. The national government had the tools to become more engaged, but either chose not to or was limited in the use of those tools by the courts. Nevertheless, although there were still vast areas where the states retained considerable governing authority, a new sense of nationalism was developing.

At the same time, an emerging national economy, rising national industrialization, with its concomitant corporate structure, and the nationalization of the economy presented questions and led to the enhancement of national power through the decisions of the Supreme Court. Building upon the three Reconstruction Amendments to the Constitution, the Court's federalism jurisprudence reflected this new nationalism.

In a notable decision handed down in 1873, the Supreme Court embraced a doctrine of dual citizenship which, in essence, left to the states much of the authority regarding the protections of individual rights. The Fourteenth Amendment cited the "privileges and immunities" of the citizens of the nation and of the states, and the Court said it was not the job of the national government, per se, to protect those "privileges and immunities." "It is quite clear that there is a citizenship of the United States and a citizenship of a state, which are distinct from each other." In the eyes of the Court, the Fourteenth Amendment did little or nothing to disturb or restrict the powers of a state to regulate private property interests within its boundaries. With dual citizenship, the Court decided there was little or no change in the relationship between the states and the national government due to the Fourteenth Amendment. In the years following, it tended to restate that position.

From the end of the Civil War until the Great Depression, the constitutional pendulum swung back and forth regarding the Court and federalism, but gradually tilted toward the national government. Through its interpretations of the Commerce Clause, Supremacy Clause, Contracts Clause, and Necessary and Proper Clause, the Court began to reshape the contours of American federalism. In 1877, it said Congress passes laws "for the whole nation, and is not embarrassed by State lines." In 1887, passing judgment on the legality and scope of the Interstate Commerce

Act, the Court asserted that the national government's policies "preempted" those of the states when the Congress sought to "occupy the field." Later, when looking at the Pure Food and Drug Act, it found the executive branch could preempt state action as well, even without explicit statutory authorization, giving birth to the notion of "implied" preemption. But a number of decisions handed down in the early 20th century seemed to buttress the states as well.

In a series of attempts to initiate social policy through the use of the Commerce Clause, Congress passed legislation dealing with such issues as child labor, minimum hours and wages, and working conditions. The Court, holding to a narrow view of the Congress's commerce powers, held that it could not ban from interstate commerce products made through child labor, finding a distinction between making products and selling them and upholding the authority of states to regulate the latter: "The power of the States to regulate their purely internal affairs by such laws as seem wise to their local authority is inherent and has never been surrendered to the general government." In *Hammer v. Dagenhart* (1918), the Court drew clear distinctions that would be revisited in the wake of the Great Depression years later:

> The making of goods and the mining of coal are not Commerce…. The production of articles intended for interstate commerce is a matter of local regulation…. If it were otherwise, all manufacture intended for interstate shipment would be brought under Federal control to the practical exclusion of the authority of the States—a result certainly not contemplated by the Framers of the Constitution.

The Court followed similar logic when it upheld the authority of states to regulate the wages and hours of employees: "If the commerce clause were construed to reach all enterprises and transaction which could be said to have an indirect effect upon interstate commerce," it opined in 1935, "the federal authority would embrace practically all the activities of the people and the authority of State over its domestic concerns would exist only by the sufferance of the federal government." (*A.L.A. Schechter Poultry Corp. v. United States* (1935)).

The political culture of the early Republic was largely defined by its identification with the states. As the century came to a close, though, it was becoming clear that the prevailing sentiment was changing. A generation of judges in the federal courts that had been generally deferential to the inherited state and national relationship was succeeded by a generation that was more inclined to seek to protect property rights. Moreover, the attitude toward the government began to change. A healthy skepticism of government and an embrace of the marketplace had produced the American industrial revolution. But as that revolution matured, more and more individuals began to look to government to become more actively engaged in regulating the economy and providing benefits to the people. It was the beginning of the Progressive Era.

Chapter 5

The Assault of Liberalism

A s the 20th century opened, Americans increasingly began to embrace a reformist mentality that led to a host of initiatives at all levels of government. Congress passed laws establishing regulation of the meat-packing industry, drugs, railroads, and agriculture. It established comprehensive federal control of the banking system, strengthened anti-trust laws, and regulated workers' conditions. At the state and local level, efforts were mounted to clean up urban political corruption, to expand education, and to end urban moral blight. States started to enact minimum wage laws, restrict child labor, and regulate factory working conditions. Numerous reforms in governing were introduced. The idea of a politically neutral civil service, first called for in the 1880s, was embraced with a number of reforms at the national level that provided the foundation for the contemporary civil service. In some cities, the city manager system was introduced in an attempt to neutralize political machines and to introduce sound management principles to the business of government.

The Progressive Movement reflected a broad embrace of a more active national government that would engage in social policy and seek to correct the perceived ills of government and society. It rejected, in many ways, the notion of a limited government of enumerated powers as inadequate to the needs of the times. The Progressives sought to empower the government to do good. An era of reform was ushered in that embraced democracy, the scientific method, and rational management techniques, while seeking to purge politics of its many alleged corruptions. It set in motion public policy prescriptions that would later bloom to full flower under Franklin Roosevelt and the New Deal and started a revolution in the nation's popular understanding of the Constitution that continues to this day.

Looking to fashion responses to many of the social ills afflicting society, these reformers sought to write public policy that would empower the government to do things that up until that time were considered well beyond anything authorized by the Constitution. Their argument was that the Constitution needed to be understood within the context of the times; its meaning needed to be adapted to changes in circumstances.

It was Woodrow Wilson, who would go on to become President, who provided much of the intellectual foundation for a new argument that the Constitution should be viewed as a "living" document, constantly evolving with the progress of society. His case for this argument can be seen most clearly in two of his early writings: *Congressional Government* (1886) and *Constitutional Government in the United States* (1908). In both books, he argued there were inherent problems and limitations with the system of government provided by the Constitution. An advocate for a system of government akin to the parliamentary model of Great Britain, Wilson argued that the equilibrium among the three branches of government made it difficult to govern and to enact policy, and to hold government accountable. The Framers' notion of a government of balanced institutions was inadequate to the needs of the times. "Government is not a machine, but a living thing," he argued. "It falls, not under the theory of the universe, but under the theory of organic life. It is accountable to Darwin."

Wilson's argument that the Constitution has meaning that evolves over time and can mean different things in different ages has become widely accepted, especially in the academy and intellectual circles. But much like the idea of the Constitution meaning only what judges say it means, to accept Wilson's principle is to render the Constitution on its own almost meaningless—or, at the very least, meaning whatever one wants it to mean. It is to embrace a notion of "constitutional relativism" that dismisses out of hand those principles of government that were central to the creation of the document.

The Framers of the Constitution never spoke of a "living" constitution but instead a permanent one. For the men who gathered in Philadelphia, words were not simply empty vessels into which one might pour meaning. For the Framers, words had meaning, and they chose their words carefully to express exactly what the Constitution was intended to provide. They recognized a need to allow for the inevitable change in society and created a mechanism for changing the Constitution accordingly. But they also saw a need to seek to temper what may be temporary popularity with adherence to permanent principles. They understood the distinction between popular impulse or inclination and the long-term public interest. They recognized the need for a written constitution that would provide "the fundamental and paramount law of the nation." It was because certain principles were considered to be of such important and permanent nature that a revolution was fought and a new government was constructed—a new government under a written constitution so that government might not stray from those principles.

The doctrine of a "living" constitution is the product not only of a misguided view of the Framers' understanding of the Constitution but also of constitutionalism as such. It has both provided the rationale and been nourished by the idea that the Constitution means only what judges say it means, thus providing a majority on the Court, from time to time, an authority the Constitution does not give them. And it has provided the intellectual, legal, and political rationale for contemporary federalism and the modern administrative state. Thus the "living

Constitution" is the necessary predicate to liberalism's practical agenda.

THE BIRTH OF THE ADMINISTRATIVE STATE

During the early part of the 20th century, the states continued to exercise broad authority in a host of areas, to be sure, but gradually a larger federal presence came to dominate American politics. The national government became engaged in providing grants to states for agricultural and irrigation projects in the West. With the Pure Food and Drug Act it became more actively engaged in the police powers traditionally left to the states. The Federal Reserve Act and the Clayton Antitrust Act greatly extended the national government's reach into the financial, economic, and business regulatory arena. Moreover, the mobilization of the nation to fight a world war served to accelerate the centralizing tendencies already underway. And while the federal courts would keep the centralizing tendency in check until confronted with an economic crisis that could not be ignored, the national government's reach soon extended to every citizen and every state. It was the beginning of the modern administrative state.

Several constitutional amendments were ratified during this time that would change forever the character of federalism in America. In 1913, the Sixteenth Amendment provided the national government with the authority to establish a national income tax. With this amendment, the national government's revenue raising power placed it at great advantage over the states. By ensuring a vast financial advantage, the income tax established forever the political advantage the national government would have over the states. With that advantage, and through its exercise of the taxing and spending powers, Washington would revolutionize the federal relationship. By employing its ability to make grants to the states to promote and implement national programs and priorities, Congress has been able to transform the states largely into administrative arms of the national government. And by attaching all sorts of conditions and regulations to the receipt of federal funds, the national government has been able to get even the most recalcitrant states to go along with its priorities.

That same year, the Seventeenth Amendment established the direct election of the United States Senate. The Senate was the "federal" branch of Congress, as James Madison had argued in *The Federalist*. Originally, senators were selected by the state legislatures to represent the interests of their states, and each state's having two senators, regardless of its size or population, was a recognition of the sovereignty each state possessed. Over time, the selection of senators by state legislators had, in many places, taken on the character of political favoritism and deal-making. Moreover, the Progressive embrace of such democratic ideas as referendum and initiative led to calls for a more democratic process for choosing senators. The Seventeenth Amendment, then, reflected the growing democratic sentiment of the American people. But it would change forever the federal character and purpose behind the Senate. The Framers had intended the Senate to reflect the need for a chamber in the national Congress that was representative of the states—a chamber that would behave differently than the House of Representatives and serve different purposes. With the Seventeenth Amendment, those differences and purposes began to dissolve.

It is difficult to overstate the impact of the Seventeenth Amendment on Congress and on federalism. On one level, it transformed Congress into a totally popular, democratic, and national institution; both chambers were now elected directly by the people. It changed the purpose and character of the Senate. Originally, equal representation of each state, regardless of population, was seen as a guarantee that the interests of each state, as a state, would be represented and respected in the national legislature. Senators were chosen, in other words, to represent states as political entities; state interests, not popular interests, were their concern. The Seventeenth Amendment did away with this principle. The Senate now served the same interests as the House, albeit it would go about it differently.

But with the Amendment, the special role that was assigned to the Senate by the Constitution—advice and consent to executive and judicial appointments, the ratification of treaties—would gradually undergo change as well. An institution designed to reflect the needs and interests of the states and the Union was transformed into an institution reflecting popular sentiment and opinion and would bring that to the deliberative process.

All of this, of course, meant the constitutional and institutional embrace of federalism so embodied by the Framers' Senate was gone. While the Senate remains a unique chamber, with its rules and procedures aimed at recognizing the essential equality of each state, its federal purpose has dried up. And an institution once designed to provide for the "cool and deliberate sense of the community" has become another popular assembly in which public opinion is weighed almost unencumbered by other political principles.

In 1920, the Nineteenth Amendment extended the franchise to women. Reflecting the democratization of the American character, the right to vote for women had been sought for decades, but had been subject to state regulation. With the Nineteenth Amendment it became a national constitutional right. But not all the Progressive amendments to the Constitution endured. The Eighteenth Amendment, establishing Prohibition, was repealed with the Twenty-first Amendment in 1933.

The centralizing tendencies of American politics and government were checked somewhat by a series of Supreme Court decisions that embraced narrow interpretations of the Commerce Clause and deferred to state regulation. The Court said that manufacturing is not commerce and labor is not commerce, and therefore limited the reach of Congress under the Commerce Clause. On the other hand, the Court began to broaden its understanding of the Fourteenth Amendment, limiting some state actions it had previously left alone. And gradually the Court began to apply some of the protections of the Bill of Rights to the states through the Fourteenth Amendment. But judicial interpretations were less influential than the changing political nature of the federal relationship. With the income tax and increased national treasury were sown the seeds that would produce the modern age of intergovernmental relations.

THE PROBLEM OF "INCORPORATION"

Over the years, the Supreme Court, in a number of cases, has held that many of the protections in the first eight amendments of the Bill of Rights are included or "incorporated" in the "liberty" and "privileges and immunities" protected by the Fourteenth Amendment Due Process Clause. This has meant that the Constitution's protections of individual rights against action by the national government also extend against state action. Simply put, the First Amendment's limits on Congress—"Congress shall make no law"—are, in the eyes of the Court, more accurately read to mean "government can make no law."

Referred to as the incorporation doctrine, there is considerable debate over whether the Court's actions reflect the intentions of those who framed and ratified the Fourteenth Amendment. There is no debate about the fact that in the pre-Civil War South, states passed laws making speech and publications critical of slavery a crime. After the War, measures were passed in the South aimed at limiting the rights and opportunities of the freed slaves, as well as others who had been loyal to the Union. This angered many in Congress, mostly Republicans, who felt that basic rights were being denied to citizens. The Fourteenth Amendment was enacted, in part, to counter such state action. But it is unclear whether its framers meant to apply the protections of the Bill of Rights to states. During the debate that led to the proposed amendment, some in Congress argued that the privileges or immunities of citizens of the United States include some or all the rights in the Bill of Rights. No one explicitly sought to contradict that argument. But most of the discussion did not focus on the question, and much of the debate seemed to challenge such an idea. While as a matter of constitutional law the general question of incorporation mostly is settled, the debate continues among legal scholars today.

In 1897, the Supreme Court made its initial determination that the Fourteenth Amendment incorporated the Bill of Rights when it found that the Fifth Amendment's guarantee that private property cannot be taken for public purpose without just compensation limited states, thereby reversing Marshall's position in *Barron*. But for many years thereafter, the Court did not expand upon the idea. Then, in 1925, in *Gitlow v. New York*, the Court said the First Amendment's protection of freedom of speech and press must be construed to limit the states as well as the national government. In a later case, the Court said that some of the privileges and immunities embraced in the Bill of Rights were so important that states were required to respect them under the Due Process Clause of the Fourteenth Amendment, while others were less important and subject to state action. The jurisprudential debate continued for years. Today, through the doctrine of incorporation, applied in a rich and diverse history of cases and controversies, the rights guaranteed in the first eight amendments of the Bill of Rights have been interpreted by the Courts to limit the states as well as Washington. The effect has been to place a heavy burden on the federal judiciary to be the arbiter of all sorts of disputes surrounding the exercise of these rights. And it has had the effect of changing forever (it would seem) the relationship of the Bill of Rights to the states. What was once understood to be a symbol of the sovereignty left to reside among the states has become a vehicle that challenges much of that sovereignty.

The incorporation doctrine, despite its questionable origins, has become a subject of legal scholarship and debate, but it is merely that—an academic debate. The Court's precedents on the application of the Bill of Rights to the states are by now beyond question. It is settled law. Few Americans would even question whether their freedom of speech pertained to state as well as national government action. Fewer still would even know that this was once not the case. But there have been other consequences accompanying incorporation that have had the effect of not only undermining federalism but altering the role of the courts in American society.

When the rights of individuals against state action were subject to state constitutional and statutory action, the debate took place within the states. One problem with this, of course, is that the laws varied among the states, much as the politics did. But this also meant citizens had to pay more attention to what their state governments did and be more engaged in securing their rights and interests. The "nationalization" of the Bill of Rights removed this burden from citizens just as it removed this authority from states.

NEW DEAL CENTRALIZATION

The modern administrative state came into full flower during the period from the Great Depression through the New Deal and World War II. The Depression, for a time, challenged the very future of the nation and its government. President Franklin Roosevelt's New Deal initiatives were aimed at getting the various sectors of the economy under national regulatory control. Areas once under state regulation were to become subject to national regulation. Proposals to regulate agriculture, manufacturing, labor, transportation, banking, securities—virtually every sector of economic activity—were put forth in a massive package of proposals to fuel an economic recovery. In a series of decisions, the Supreme Court struck down Roosevelt's initiatives.

Roosevelt, during his first hundred days in office, had asserted that the Constitution "can always meet extraordinary needs" and put forth a series of legislative and regulatory proposals aimed at ending the Depression. Among these were the National Industrial

Recovery Act of 1933 and the Agricultural Adjustment Act. The Court initially upheld a number of Roosevelt's New Deal initiatives. But it struck down both the National Industrial Recovery Act and the Agricultural Adjustment Act, as well at some state regulatory efforts aimed at economic recovery.

As such, the Court's decisions stood in the way of Roosevelt's reform program and were widely seen as harkening back to an earlier era, blind to the economic catastrophe confronting the nation. In 1937, the President hatched his plan to "pack the Court" by expanding its size so as to be able to appoint justices more supportive of his New Deal policies. The plan was never implemented, but the threat of it happening—along with the growing case for a new liberal jurisprudence—had the effect Roosevelt had sought. The Court began to overturn earlier holdings and embrace the New Deal. With *West Coast Hotel v. Parrish* (1937) it signaled its willingness to accept state and federal regulatory legislation. With subsequent cases it dismantled its "laissez-faire constitutionalism," substantive due process, and freedom of contract. With the retirement of justices and the subsequent appointment of new ones by Roosevelt, the President was able to cement not only his New Deal program but also an expansionist judicial philosophy in the court. This era witnessed an unprecedented national expansion into every aspect of American life, amounting to what can be called a constitutional revolution.

In a series of cases, the Court upheld a number of New Deal initiatives, giving birth to the modern administrative state, finding old distinctions blurred, and reading expansive new authority in the Commerce Clause of the Constitution while all but quieting the Tenth Amendment. In upholding federal minimum wage laws in 1941 (*United States v. Darby Lumber*), the Court said that the Tenth Amendment "states but a truism that all is retained which had not been surrendered." Thus the Court ended its protective defense of the doctrine of federalism.

With *Wickard v. Filburn* (1942), the justices completed their rewriting of earlier Commerce Clause thinking. Suddenly, whether something was manufactured for interstate commerce or not, it was subject to federal regulation—even wheat grown by a farmer for his own consumption.

> Whether the subject of regulation in question was "production," "consumption," or "marketing" is, therefore, not material for purposes of deciding the question of federal power before us.... But even if the appellee's activity be local and though it may not be regarded as commerce, it may still, whatever its nature, be reached by Congress if it exerts a substantial economic interest on interstate commerce....

With *Wickard*, the Court reaffirmed not only the New Deal but the nationalization of the economy that was transpiring during the 20th century. Since then, the centralization of governmental authority has continued. Through the doctrine of incorporation, the reach of the protections in the Bill of Rights has been extended. Expansive interpretations of the Commerce Clause have enabled Congress to regulate state activity and social policy. The scope of the national government's authority to manage issues relating to civil rights has been extended to even the most local of issues. And the ability of states to determine the contours and character of their own governmental institutions has been limited. Finding that "political subdivisions of States...never were and never have been considered as sovereign entities," the Court established a new constitutional principle to govern what state legislatures must look like, thus rewriting many state constitutions.

> We hold that, as a basic constitutional standard, the Equal Protection clause requires that the seats in both houses of a bicameral state legislature must be apportioned on a population basis.

During this time, the Tenth Amendment of the Constitution—the "federalism" amendment—has been all but ignored by the Court. Only briefly, in 1976, was it employed to protect the ability of states to regulate the working conditions of their employees, a decision overturned within a decade. In recent years, a more conservative Court has revisited the Congress's Commerce Clause authority and breathed some new life into constitutional federalism. And Congress has balked at the Court seeing limits to its authority.

It would be simplistic and incorrect to argue that the "constitutional revolution" of the New Deal was due solely to the politics of the day and the pressure on the Court applied by Roosevelt. The changes were brought about by the gradual triumph of one set of ideas over another. A limited constitution was replaced by an empowering one. The broad popular understanding of the Constitution embodying certain permanent principles was replaced over time by the notion of a "living" Constitution whose meaning might change over time. With this, the courts became "problem solvers," just like their elected counterparts, and any sense of limitations imposed by the Constitution gave way to an open-ended belief in judicial public policy making.

The nature of government in America was transformed during this time in the nation's history. A general mistrust and skepticism of government had informed the framing of the Constitution in 1787. Government at all levels needed to be limited and its powers enumerated. The new national government was checked by the very structures of government created by the Constitution and by the states. It was all about a competent but limited national government. For generations, the political and constitutional debate revolved around the nature of those checks and what a competent national government might look like. With the consolidation, centralization, and expansion of the national government during the 20th century, the American governing philosophy reflected an embrace of government as a vehicle to correct economic, social, moral, and political problems. A limited government was transformed into an activist government. A government of limited powers was transformed into a government of almost unlimited scope. With this, the idea of federalism that seemed to dominate the early political life of the Republic was turned on its head. The states, though surely retaining governing authority over a host of issues within their borders, took on the role as administrators for national programs enacted in Washington, underwritten by national tax dollars, and implemented at the state and local level.

The Progressive Movement provided the intellectual foundation for the transformation of the Constitution that took place in the 1930s and 1940s. The Great Depression and the New Deal provided the economic and political impetus to see the transformation through. And it was completed during the last half of the century, as the consolidation of the role and scope of the national government continued, effectively paring back if not eliminating completely any limits on that government while producing a judiciary every bit as powerful in policy and politics as the other two branches of government.

GREAT SOCIETY LIBERALISM AND ITS CRITICS

During the 1960s, President Lyndon Johnson's Great Society proposals sought to expand the legacy of the New Deal even more, with major national initiatives in education, housing, transportation, urban renewal, and poverty. Through the use of grants and the creation of a huge national bureaucracy, Johnson sought to transform the nation through yet another enhancement of the role and power of the national government. While many, if not most, of Johnson's initiatives failed to accomplish the noble purposes he sought to promote—to win a "war on poverty," for example—much of the administrative state, its bureaucratic operators and numerous programs created during his tenure, remains in Washington. Attempts by succeeding Presidents have not done much to reshape the political or administrative landscape.

Richard Nixon's New Federalism rearranged the grant-in-aid process somewhat and sought to provide greater administrative flexibility for states engaged in the exercise of intergovernmental affairs. But he was unable to rewrite national–state relationships. For Johnson, the Vietnam war defeated his domestic visions. For Nixon, Watergate ended his chances for achieving fundamental change in both federal and international relations. President Jimmy Carter, inheriting an energy crisis and, in the end, conquered by an international crisis, did little to alter the nature of federalism, creating two new national Cabinet-level agencies and continuing the growth of the national administrative state.

When Ronald Reagan ran for the presidency, he put forth the principle that government was the source of many of the problems confronting the country rather than the answer to those problems. He called for reducing the size and reach of the national government. Throughout his Administration, Reagan continued to embrace this theme. But by the time he left office, the size of the national government and its budget were greater than ever in history. None of Reagan's successors embraced his anti-government rhetoric while each has overseen ongoing growth in government. Curiously, President George W. Bush, while fashioning himself a conservative, successfully enacted broad reform in public education that expanded national authority into the local classroom as never before. And in response to threats of terrorism and natural disasters, he oversaw bold new initiatives that broadened even more the role of the national government.

Against this backdrop, then, contemporary federalism bears little resemblance to the principle that first appeared during that summer in 1787. Today's is a federalism that establishes the all but unquestioned supremacy of the national government in almost every aspect of the nation's life. It is a federalism that looks to the states for the administration of government policy emanating from

Washington even more than from the state capital—a federalism that too often has reduced governors to supplicants seeking relief at the hands of Washington. It is a federalism composed of an intricate web of policies and procedures, rules and regulations, and billions of dollars flowing back and forth from Washington to each state. It is a federalism reflective of, and contributing to, the modern American administrative state.

The great problem, of course, is that it is a federalism that has lost touch with its original purposes, altering not only the nature of government and politics in America, but the character of America itself.

Chapter 6

The Challenge
of Federalism

I n theory and design, the Constitution is a conservative
document. It creates a national government and outlines the
powers of that government. To this extent, it is an empowering
document. But it is a conservative document in that the powers
given the national government are enumerated; the government
cannot do what the Constitution does not authorize it to do.
Moreover, the very structure of the national government, as
outlined in the Constitution, is designed to make it relatively
difficult for the government to do much of anything. Separation of
powers, checks and balances, and federalism combine to create
obstacles to action that must be overcome in order for the national
government to act. A sort of creative tension among the branches
of government and among governments is established by the
Constitution; no single branch within government and no single
government (federal or state) is to gain the advantage. Contrary to
contemporary popular sentiment, the Constitution is not designed
to facilitate policymaking at the national level. Indeed, it is
designed to render policymaking relatively difficult.

All of this seems quite at odds, of course, with the nature of
government in modern America. As we have seen, over the scope of
the nation's history, the theory of government embraced by the
Framers of the Constitution seems to have been turned on its

head. The powers of the states, once thought sovereign, have been undermined by a seemingly all-powerful national government that seems to have virtually unlimited authority. The Bill of Rights, once considered a vehicle for protecting both individual rights and state governments from national action, has been transformed into a vehicle for not only protecting rights but creating new ones, while simultaneously limiting state as well as national action. It seems that the Constitution bestows vast authority upon Congress, the President, and the Supreme Court.

The apparent chasm between the Constitution in theory and the Constitution as it has evolved can be attributed to the changing needs and opportunities that have marked over two centuries of American political, legal, and constitutional history and development. What was once the subject of sometimes bitter dispute— say, the authority of the national government to provide for internal improvements such as highways—is now accepted as commonplace and beyond question. Moreover, our popular understanding of what we expect from our national government varies greatly from that which informed those who created it in the 18th century. The Framers were healthy skeptics of government; we seem to embrace it, albeit with some skepticism as well. While we continuously criticize government, we tend to turn to it for almost everything, from disaster relief to education, health care to transportation.

Given all this, it might be understandable that most Americans know little about the animating theories and principles that underlie their Constitution. Things that once mattered a great deal seem somehow less than relevant in modern America. But that is the point. For while the Framers expected the Constitution and the government it created to change with the times, they also expected the principles embraced by the document to help guide those changes. Federalism, for example, meant that the authority of the states cannot be ignored even while it might change with time and circumstance. That was the point behind having a written constitution in the first place. As one scholar has phrased it, the point was not to keep the Constitution in touch with the times but to keep the times in touch with the Constitution.

It seems almost quaint by today's standards to assert that the Constitution established a limited national government. But the Framers sought to establish a government that would do a few things well. Even the most ardent nationalists of the 18th and early 19th centuries sought a competent but somewhat limited national government. More broadly, federalism was considered essential to the maintenance of limited government, the protection of individual rights and liberty, and the cultivation of good citizenship. To the extent that it has eroded as a constitutional and political principle, the way government operates, the way rights are safeguarded, and the nature of citizenship in America have changed as well.

GOVERNMENT BY JUDICIARY

All this began to change, as we have seen, as the nation expanded, its economy grew, and the government was forced to grapple with issues that seemed to render notions of limited government antiquated. Judicial interpretations of the Constitution gradually reflected the times as well, even when some of those interpretations seemed completely at odds with the text of the Constitution itself. How else can one explain the contemporary meaning of the Commerce Clause, or the authority of unelected federal bureaucrats to override state policies, laws, and regulations through the idea of "implied preemption"? So the Constitution today is very different, in both its meaning and effect, from the vision of those who wrote it. And federalism is a mere shadow of its former self. Much of the rationale for this fundamental change in our popular understanding of the Constitution and the government created by it can be found in the notion of the Constitution as a "living" document.

Unfortunately, it is not just a commonplace but a doctrine that the Constitution is a "living" document. High school students are taught that the Constitution "adapts" to changes in time and circumstance much the way an organism adjusts to changes in its environment. Students enrolled in undergraduate courses in American government are told the Constitution remains relevant primarily because of the efforts of politicians and judges to "interpret" the document and "bend" it to fit contemporary circumstances. Budding young lawyers are taught constitutional law by reading Supreme Court decisions and learn how the Court seeks to interpret the Constitution in light of changing meaning to fit changing times. It is a "living" constitution, so it is argued, not only because it specifies the governmental "rules of the game," but because it also "encompasses implicit norms of custom and usage, which have evolved over the decades in response to important political needs."

The doctrine of a "living" constitution is the byproduct of two themes in constitutional development. The first is the notion that the Constitution is, as Chief Justice Charles Evans Hughes once put it "what the judges say it is." It is the idea that the meaning of the document is decided by the courts—that judicial decisions are the Constitution. The second is the idea that the Constitution is best understood within the context of Darwinian principles rather than Newtonian ones; it is about an organism needing to adapt to changes in its environment rather than balancing institutions of government.

Reducing the Constitution to nothing other than judicial opinion is tantamount to saying the document can have no meaning other than that decided by a court. This is at odds with much of the nation's history. While the courts have always played an important role in constitutional debates, and since *Marbury v. Madison* (1803) have been the chief arbiters of constitutional interpretation, it is a somewhat dangerous leap to suggest that the nation's fundamental governing document only means what a few judges say it means. While we have relied upon courts to resolve constitutional disputes, the fact that such disputes take place suggests that understandings of the Constitution independent of those rendered by the judiciary are commonplace. Moreover, our nation's history is replete with examples of constitutional interpretation independent of judicial opinion. Calhoun's resort to a theory of nullification is an example. No court ever spoke to it. Rather it was a debate between rivals over the meaning of the Constitution, federalism, and the Union. Ultimately it took a war to settle the dispute. Throughout, the judiciary remained silent.

A greater problem with reducing the meaning of the Constitution to whatever the Court says it means is that it makes it all but impossible for the Court to be wrong. Clearly, however, it has been wrong from time to time. How else can one explain how the Court can find segregation constitutional at one point and unconstitutional at another? The words of the Constitution did not change in the interim. The makeup of the Court did change, however, as did the times. The Court in *Brown v. Board of Education* (1954) found the reasoning of the *Plessy v. Ferguson* (1896) Court to be wrong, for example. But it becomes impossible to evaluate the quality of the Court's constitutional decisions if its decisions define, de facto, what the Constitution means. And it reduces the meaning of the Constitution to mere judicial opinion, as if the words might have no meaning on their own. Commerce means whatever a judge says it means. Clearly this is at odds with what the Framers of the Constitution intended. They chose their words carefully and for good reasons. Finally, to admit the Constitution has meaning only through judicial interpretation is to forget that the Constitution was meant to govern the judiciary as well as the other branches of government. To think otherwise is to lay the foundation for a government by judiciary that is inconsistent with the very idea of having a written constitution to begin with.

The Court's understanding of federalism as a constitutional principle has, over time, reflected its understanding of both the Constitution and the demands of a growing and changing nation. The idea of a strict regard for the sovereignty of the states has been replaced with a due respect for the states partnered with a healthy embrace of the authority of the national government. It is this notion of federalism that recognizes the role of the national government in the daily affairs of citizens and in the world at large. And it is an understanding of federalism that would seem quite at odds with the understanding embraced by those who wrote the Constitution. This makes some sense. The nation and the world have changed in dramatic and fundamental ways since the creation of the Constitution, and the way the states relate to one another and to the government in Washington surely has to change over time as well. But there have been costs associated with the Court's having all but abandoned federalism.

The Supreme Court's gradual embrace of a consolidated and energetic national government, while perhaps necessary in some respects, has surely undermined an important practical aspect of American federalism. It is more than coincidental that the emergence of the modern administrative state has been accompanied by a decline in civic participation, public confidence in government, and electoral participation. Surely there are many explanations for all of this. But federalism was once seen as a way to keep Americans in touch with their governments. The degree to which it has faded as a constitutional and governing principle in this country might help to explain why Americans feel the way they do about government and politics today. And a deeper appreciation for the principle of federalism might provide some antidotes to the political afflictions so common in modern America.

THE RIGHTS REVOLUTION

As federalism has evolved over time, the role of the states in American government and politics has been altered. Perhaps this is most obvious in the changed relationship of the states to the national government regarding the protection of individual rights. What was originally intended to be a check upon the powers of the national government—the Bill of Rights—has been transformed into a vehicle that has enhanced the power of the national government in the name of protecting individual rights. It is surely one of the ironies of our constitutional history that an entire portion of the Constitution dedicated to the preservation of individual liberties through the maintenance of a limited government has produced instead an expansive national government. In retrospect, the fears of the Anti-Federalists seem all too prescient. As Raoul Berger wrote in *Government by Judiciary*, "it was not the fear of State mismanagement but distrust of the remote federal newcomer that fueled the demand for a federal Bill of Rights which would supply the same protections against the federal government that State constitutions already provided against the States." Be that as it may, today Americans turn to Washington, and with greater frequency, to the federal courts, for the protection of their rights and liberties. The rules of the constitutional game have changed. Most Americans seem quite comfortable with things as they stand today. But what is troubling is the kind of thinking that produced such a major transformation in the relationship of the individual to his government.

While it may indeed be desirable to establish a rule of law for civil rights and liberties that is, as Henry Abraham states in *Freedom and the Court*, "both drastic and simple and that would guarantee certainty for all future litigation," the reasoning that went into establishing such a rule is questionable. Moreover, it altered forever how men and women think about government in America. Today they look to government not only to protect rights but to create and extend them. They turn to federal courts to provide what Congress and state legislatures do not provide, wrapping arguments to advance various interests in the cloak of advocating rights and freedoms, thereby enhancing even more the authority of the courts while undermining the efficacy of the political branches and the states. In the process, the old distinctions between rights, interests, and entitlements become blurred. It seems at times that

America has become obsessed with rights. Political discourse today is so much "rights talk," as individuals and groups assert their rights against one another and the government. Moreover, a concern with individual rights has been displaced with a concern for group rights, asserted by groups that argue the need to correct for alleged past wrongs. The very idea of self-government begins to get bogged down in a morass of litigation and politics.

This shift to group as opposed to individual rights is at odds with the theory of rights embraced in the Declaration of Independence and the Constitution. There is a theory of rights possessed by all individuals equally. It is a theory that asserts what everyone has in common. The assertion of group rights involves claims being made by one group against another, which invariably involves inequalities and making distinctions among people. It is an approach to rights which forces people to dwell on what they do not have in common, undermining any deeper sense of community that might come to shape the contours of our politics. The emphasis on group rights renders any distinctions between rights, interests and entitlements almost negligible. Today it is commonplace to hear of a right to a job, to health care, to education, to welfare benefits, etc. An earlier generation would have framed such issues in the context of political interests, not rights. It is in the public interest to promote employment, education, help for the needy, etc. Gradually, however, as generations have come to expect such programs from government, they have come to depend upon them—as though they have a right to them—thereby shifting the terms of the political discourse and the focus of debate. Suddenly, what are now regarded as rights are things people seek from and receive from government as opposed to something individuals possess by nature and governments are instituted to secure.

During the second half of the 20th century, the national government became directly engaged in the protection of civil rights. In *Plessy v. Ferguson* (1896), the Court had found states could maintain separate facilities for blacks and whites, thus upholding the doctrine of segregation in almost all of the South. With *Brown v. Board of Education* (1954), the Supreme Court reversed precedent and found the doctrine of racial segregation in education unconstitutional, arguing that "separate educational facilities are inherently unequal." The decision ushered in an era of civil rights and racial strife that led to protections for voting, accommodations, and employment. Each of these required national legislation, judicial interpretation, and national enforcement. All three branches of the national government contributed to the civil rights expansion. Those Americans long denied their rights under state action, primarily though not exclusively in the South, now looked to Washington for the protection of those rights. And they turned to the federal courts to determine the contours of those rights.

A deeper and more troubling consequence of shifting the responsibility to the federal courts as final arbiters of individual rights vis-à-vis government has been the judiciary's tendency to create rights as it seeks to interpret the Constitution and arbitrate legitimate disputes. No line of cases illustrates this better than those which began in 1965 and continue to the present time.

In *Griswold v. Connecticut* (1965), the Supreme Court found unconstitutional a Connecticut law prohibiting the use of contraceptives. In doing this, the Court found that there was a right of reproductive privacy in the Bill of Rights and that Connecticut was, therefore, violating the Due Process Clause of the Fourteenth Amendment. In what has become an oft-cited passage from the majority decision of the Court, this right of privacy was to be found in the "penumbras formed by emanations" from the Bill of Rights. This decision laid the judicial and constitutional foundation for the Court's most controversial decision in a generation—*Roe v. Wade* (1973)—in which the Court held that an unborn child is not a person for the purposes of the Fourteenth Amendment and that the right of privacy prevents states from prohibiting abortions. This decision, and a series of decisions since it was handed down, have become the focus of an ongoing national debate on how to interpret the Constitution and the Bill of Rights and the nature and scope of judicial power.

Putting aside the issue of abortion, what was once a debate among citizens, voters, elected officials, and state courts has become almost exclusively a debate within the federal courts. Similarly, the development of public policy in such areas as capital punishment, school prayer, search and seizure, self-incrimination, pornography, and homosexual activity has been all but removed from state authority and become the responsibility of the federal courts. What was once the responsibility of elected officials has become the responsibility of non-elected federal judges. It has become the product of legal and judicial discussion, with elected officials and the citizens they represent relegated to the sidelines as interested and affected observers. Again, putting the specific policies aside, that has had a deleterious effect upon the quality of our state and national political discourse, undermined the authority of the states under the Constitution, and greatly expanded the role of the courts in American society.

For those who supported and those who opposed the Constitution in 1787, rights were important. They agreed that governments are created to secure individual rights. For the Anti-Federalists, the best way to secure rights was through state constitutions and an active and informed citizenry. Citizens protect rights because they control government. It is a theory of rights that recognized a citizen's responsibility to protect rights, as well as a governmental responsibility. Indeed, it was a theory that recognized the citizen and the government as inextricably interrelated— self-government in its purest sense. The creation of a new national government represented something of a threat, not just to the states, but to self-government, and therefore to individual rights. Hence a national bill of rights was sought to protect both. Federalism, as conceived by both the Federalists and the Anti-Federalists, and which helped to produce that Bill of Rights, was understood to be a means of maintaining the political vitality of the people and the communities in which they resided while helping to secure individual liberty. It could provide a way to offset the obvious disadvantages accompanying the new, distant national government. Federalism was understood as a means for nurturing the relationship between the individual and the government, to the benefit and security of both. Federalism was a way to nourish citizenship and self-government and to protect individual rights. As it has evolved over time, federalism has become little more than a framework in which to conduct the operations of government. Protecting rights has become the exclusive province of the judiciary. And sometimes it seems the highest calling for a citizen is to take another to court.

SELF-GOVERNMENT AND CIVIC VIRTUE

When the idea was born in Philadelphia in the summer of 1787, federalism was seen not only as a way to check national power with state sovereignty, but also as a way to keep government at every level in check. Citizens, active in state and local affairs, would keep state and local governments in their place, and states would do the same thing with the new national government. As a system, federalism would have a salutary effect upon citizenship, nurturing it and encouraging self-government as it simultaneously kept the power of government in its place. Perhaps because the Framers of the Constitution knew that the nature of federalism would change over time, they understood that, in the end, good government required not only a limited government of competent powers but also active, informed, and engaged citizens. Federalism, it was thought, would encourage the formation of such citizens.

Indeed, it may be that federalism's most important contribution to constitutional government in this country is its role in nurturing and sustaining self-government and good citizenship, essential but difficult tasks in any republic. In a liberal democratic society such as the United States, individuals are free, by and large, to fashion their own brand of participatory citizenship. Because all individuals possess natural rights, no special obligations are placed upon them and relatively few special rights or privileges are awarded to them. Citizenship in the United States, in other words, may mean a great deal or very little indeed; it is pretty much up to the individual. The paradox of this, however, is that a healthy republic relies upon citizens for both direction and support.

The advent of the modern administrative state, accompanied by the transformation of federalism, the growth in government at every level, and the increased expectations of the American people, have combined to contribute to a transformation in the character of citizenship in America. A nation of citizens who make responsible choices and elect individuals to make responsible choices has been transformed into a nation of consumers of government who pay tax dollars to purchase more and more government-delivered goods and services. Individual citizens who once were agents for change in society and in government have become passive subjects of an immense nation-state. Today, it is commonplace for people to look to the government for relief from the most ordinary of concerns, support for the most basic kinds of endeavors, and vindication for the most elementary of damages. People have become clients of the state as opposed to the masters of it. They have become dependent upon government rather than government being dependent upon them.

The education reforms introduced by President George W. Bush and embraced with strong bipartisan support in Congress provide a nice illustration of what is happening to the American character. Education has always been a state and local issue. Even as Washington allocates more money than ever in support of elementary and secondary education, about 90 percent of what is spent on public education in a state is revenue generated at the state and local level. The rules governing public education are, by and large, state and local rules. The decisions on the day-to-day operations of America's public schools are driven at the local level. The problem is that America's schools are not doing a very good job. Indicators such as test scores tell us our students and schools are just not performing well and that there are real "achievement gaps" among student groups, with minority and low-income students trailing their white counterparts. American public education is not working as well as it should—as it must.

President Bush asked Congress to enact new national legislation that requires each state to enact higher academic standards for students, regulations ensuring teachers are "highly qualified," and policies to test every student in grades 3 through 8 annually, and to hold schools accountable for the performance of their students. He also asked Congress to increase federal spending for America's schools, and Congress went along. Today, the national government plays a much larger role in the administration, oversight, and governance of America's public schools. It is a bit early to know whether the schools, the students, and the nation will be better off.

But we do know some things. As the 21st century dawns in America, its citizens have turned to government to do something they once did for themselves. Recognizing that their schools are not getting the job done, they looked to Washington to do something about it. They wanted more from their schools and their students and their teachers, and so they looked to Washington to pass a law to require more from their schools and their students and their teachers. None of this is necessary, of course. It shouldn't take an act of Congress to set high standards for schools. It shouldn't take an act of Congress to hold a public school accountable to the public. But in 21st century America, public education has become something government provides rather than something the "public" or the "people" provide; public education has been transformed into government schooling. It is something people expect from their government and purchase from it with their tax dollars. It is as though the public is no longer really a part of public education.

This transformation in the character of America and in American citizenship, illustrated by the education reforms noted above, is the result of many things. And it has transpired over time, surely. But interestingly, it is a transformation that those who created the American Republic anticipated and sought to avoid, in part through federalism. They recognized that good government would depend on both the structure of the government and the civic virtue of the people. Federalism, as we have seen, was considered one way to achieve both.

Federalism's contribution to the structure of government served two purposes initially. It provided another check on the consolidation of power in the national government while ensuring the vitality of state and local government. The vitality of state and local government was considered important, as well, to nurturing the sort of civic virtue so necessary to the creation of good citizens and the maintenance of good government.

Citizenship is all about self-government: people actively participating in the public affairs of their communities and states. As this happens, the tendency all people have to pursue their own individual self-interests is blunted by a concern for a wider general civic responsibility. Managing the tension that can exist between individual self-interest and the community or public interest is particularly important in America, where the emphasis is on rights rather than individual responsibilities. Here, in order for popular government to succeed, there would be a need to ensure that there were public-spirited citizens, thus making the cultivation and nurturing of civic virtue all the more important. There would be citizens interacting with one another in the discussion and pursuit of public issues within a community in which every citizen recognizes his well-being is related to the well-being of his fellow citizens. If civic virtue is the foundation on which citizenship is built, then federalism is the crucial structure for nurturing good citizenship.

Government alone—government at any level—cannot do the job, however. Other institutions in society are important to the fashioning of a sense of civic spirit among people. Religious institutions surely are important, as are civic and community and business and trade associations. Originally, community public schools and colleges and universities were important to the formation of civic spirit. These institutions bring individuals together to share mutual interests, and in so doing also temper individual self-interest. Every week the Kiwanis Club meets for lunch, and for that hour it's about the Club and the community it serves, not the concerns of the individual members of the Club. The community's public schools are the public's property, where people gather to discuss community issues, not merely places where kids are dropped off in the morning and picked up in the afternoon.

Surely there is something almost romantic, if not just naïve, in such a vision. But for those who created the American Republic, good citizenship seemed essential to the future of that Republic. James Madison, often revered as the "Father of the Constitution," went so far as to argue that "to suppose any form of government will secure liberty or happiness without virtue in the people is a chimerical idea." John Adams, writing to Mercy Warren in 1788, argued that if virtue, "the only foundation of a free government cannot be inspired in our people, in a greater measure than they have it now, they may change their rulers, and their form of government, but they will not obtain a lasting liberty." And as the Republic became bigger and more commercial, good citizenship became even more important, thereby rendering a healthy regard for federalism more important.

Writing in the 1830s, Alexis de Tocqueville saw just how important federalism was to the political health of the nation he was visiting. Part of what captured his attention was that within this huge nation were countless communities within the states— communities in which citizens participated with one another in self-government. They were communities nourished, he noted, by civic associations, religious and charitable organizations, business groups, local newspapers, and political parties. They were communities which erected public schools and taught the importance of political and civic responsibility in those schools.

According to Tocqueville, America seemed successful at balancing individual self-interest with citizenship and community spirit, at least in part because of the federal structure of the government. It was the vitality of local government that especially impressed him. It was through local government that individuals were drawn into public affairs and a sense of community was instilled that seemed to moderate the natural tendency to pursue one's self-interest. Local institutions placed liberty

> within the peoples' reach. Local liberties which induce a great number of citizens to value the affection of kindred and neighbors, bring men constantly into contact, despite the instincts which separate them, and force them to help one another.

The federal system and vital local government, according to Tocqueville, promoted a type of patriotism or civic virtue that "in the end becomes, in a sense, mingled with personal interest." The citizen, he observed, comes to view his nation's prosperity "first as a thing useful to him and then as something he created." It is a civic virtue born of enlightened self-interest and, in Tocqueville's eyes, it was the great virtue of American government.

Tocqueville identified two factors which were critical to the maintenance of this public spirit in America: active local governments in a federal system and a belief on the part of the people that they are free to be the masters of their own fate. An individual's belief in himself seemed to matter as much as his commitment to community.

In a particularly moving and prescient passage in *Democracy in America*, Tocqueville warned that it would be difficult for America to maintain the balance it had achieved through federalism. Citing a unique sort of despotism that tends to undermine democracies, he warned of the dangers that accompany the centralization and consolidation of government. Seeking to "trace the novel features under which despotism may appear," he wrote that "the first thing that strikes the observation is an innumerable multitude of men, all equal and alike, incessantly endeavoring to procure the petty and paltry pleasures with which they glut their lives." He sees the potential for a nation of strangers—individuals so self-interested and self-involved as to be indifferent to the fate of others or of the state. It is a nation in which the individual "exists but in himself and for himself alone; and if his kindred still remain to him, he may be said at any rate to have lost his country." It is a vision of a nation in which individuals are governed by the state as opposed to the state governed by them.

> Above this race of men stands an immense and tutelary power, which takes upon itself to secure their gratifications, and to watch over their fate. The power is absolute, minute, regular, provident, and mild. It would be like the authority of a parent, if, like that authority, its object was to prepare men for manhood; but it seeks, on the contrary, to keep them in perpetual childhood: it is well content that the people should rejoice, provided they think of nothing but rejoicing. For their happiness such a government willingly labors, but it chooses to be the sole agent and the only arbiter of that happiness; it provides for their security, foresees and supplies their necessities, facilitates their pleasures, manages their principal concerns, directs their industry, regulates the descent of property, subdivides their inheritances: What remains, but to spare them all the care of thinking and all the trouble of learning?

Such a government, argued Tocqueville, "renders the exercise of the free agency of man less useful and less frequent" and "gradually robs a man of all the uses of himself." It is a government that promotes individual self-interest because it caters to it; a government that weakens the spirit of individuals and communities, leading to a decline in community and citizenship because the people no longer care. They no longer care because the government is doing what needs to be done. It is a transformation in the minds of men that is brought about by the nature of government. The despotism Tocqueville warns of is a tyranny of men's minds, as citizens no longer practice citizenship while they reside in communities in which there are no neighbors.

It is beyond ironic that while we live at a time in which our ability to communicate with one another and with people around the world is greater than ever before, we feel somehow separate and apart from events as they transpire. We possess the technology to enable every American to participate directly in public affairs. Yet, we have become more and more a society that chooses to observe rather than participate. We live in an information age and know more about more things than ever before in world history. And as our knowledge of government and politics has increased so has our distrust, doubt, and cynicism toward both.

There are, of course, several explanations for all of this. But surely a root cause of our current civic disposition is the sense that our nation's government is somehow disconnected and apart from our nation's people. It is as though government is something one reads about in newspapers, hears about on radio and television, and something to pay attention to only when directly affected by some act or decision. Government seems to "just keep on going," grinding out public policy on every conceivable issue at a snail's pace, usurping the nation's resources and spending the nation's wealth in record amounts. Elections, considered by those who created the Republic to be essential to the maintenance and nourishment of free institutions of government, have become spectacles of negativism that feed an already cynical public's cynicism, and seem to produce little turnover among elected officials and deep divisions among voters. In America today, elections don't refresh the voter's relationship with his government; they diminish that relationship.

As Tocqueville so eloquently warned, it has become increasingly difficult to maintain the democratic spirit that is so essential to the maintenance of the Great Republic. That spirit, which is measured not only in voter turnout, but in public participation in the practice of self-government, must continue to animate the sentiments of Americans in order for America to thrive. And so it is ironic that as the nation's government has acquired unprecedented domestic and international influence, it seems to be crushing those democratic sentiments that make self-government possible. But just as Tocqueville foresaw such a development, he also understood how to counter it: a nation of states and communities in which men and women engage in the practice of self-government.

Federalism was all about keeping government within the reach of the individual. It was all about keeping government in its place. It was all about the maintenance of the democratic sentiment. As federalism has diminished as a constitutional, governmental, and political principle, much that makes this nation what it is has been is put at risk. And our ability to restore the primacy of federalism in America may well shape what this nation is to become.

Selected Bibliography

Berger, Raoul. *Federalism: The Founders' Design.* This is the best account of what the authors of the Constitution had in mind regarding the debate over national versus state authority. Berger's scholarship is beyond question and his analysis sparkles with simple eloquence in unmatched insight. This is an essential book on federalism.

Berger, Raoul. *The Fourteenth Amendment and the Bill of Rights.* In this book, Berger analyzes the debate surrounding the doctrine of incorporation and, subjected to his withering scholarship, it doesn't hold up well. He revisits the scholarly debate between legal scholars Crosskey and Fairman that animated jurisprudential discourse during the 1950s. His own analysis of the debates over the Fourteenth Amendment that transpired in Congress and during its ratification reveals an amendment of limited purpose and scope. This is solid scholarship, like it or not. And a must read for those seeking to understand better the relationship of the Bill of Rights to American law and politics.

Berger, Raoul. *Government by Judiciary: The Transformation of the Fourteenth Amendment.* Here Berger relates how the courts have come to dominate American law, politics, and society through their interpretation of the Constitution's Fourteenth Amendment. This book places contemporary debates surrounding judicial confirmations in context by explaining what is at stake in judicial appointments, why, and how it has come to this.

Hamilton, Alexander, *et al.* *The Federalist.* This is obviously essential reading for anyone interested in the roots of American federalism and constitutional government. *Federalist* Numbers 44–47 specifically address federalism.

Diamond, Martin. "What the Framers Meant by Federalism" in *As Far as Republican Principles Will Admit.* Martin Diamond is one of the key scholars responsible, in the 1960s and 1970s, for reviving the serious study of the American Founding, and in particular the study of *The Federalist.* This particular essay, among his many on the topic, is the classic explanation and defense of Madison's theory that a large commercial republic is the solution to the problems inherent in small and weak republics.

Kelly, Alfred H., Winfrid A. Harbison, and Herman Belz. *The American Constitution.* For years, this was the definitive constitutional political history on the subject. It has its shortcomings but has withstood the test of time.

Madison, James. *Notes of the Debates in the Federal Convention of 1787.* This volume, among those that trace the arguments that transpired in Philadelphia in 1787, is Madison's voice telling his story. For this reason it demands attention and respect, while also inviting attention to other chroniclers of the Convention.

Storing, Herbert. *What the ANTI-FEDERALISTS Were FOR.* This fine extended essay captures the arguments of those who were opposed to the new Constitution. What impresses the reader most is how prescient some of their concerns were, given contemporary American law and politics.

Wilson, Woodrow. *Constitutional Government.* Written before he became President, this book traces Wilson's argument for a parliamentary system of government based on the British model and rooted in an understanding of the Constitution as a "living" document. Reading it, one can gain some insight into why Wilson's administration encountered the problems it did.

About the Author

Educated at Hampden-Sydney College in Virginia, Eugene W. Hickok received his master's and Ph.D. from the University of Virginia. Dr. Hickok taught political science at Dickinson College in Carlisle, Pennsylvania, and served as director of the college's Clarke Center for the Interdisciplinary Study of Contemporary Issues. He also was an adjunct professor at the Dickinson School of Law. He was recognized as an outstanding teacher and was awarded Dickinson's prestigious Ganoe Award for Inspirational Teaching in 1985 and 1990.

His extensive career in education policy led to his appointment as Pennsylvania's Secretary of Education and service on the boards of trustees of Pennsylvania's four state-related universities and on the State System of Higher Education's Board of Governors. He was also a founding member and chairman of the Education Leaders Council, a group of reform-minded education chiefs who oversee 30 percent of the nation's K–12 public school students. In 2004, Hickok was appointed U.S. Deputy Secretary of Education after having served as the Under Secretary of Education.

Dr. Hickok currently serves as an adjunct professor of political science at the University of Richmond, and is a Bradley Fellow at The Heritage Foundation. Dr. Hickok and his wife Kathy have two children and reside in Richmond, Virginia.